To Eli[...]

A ledy [...]

to the world, of great

importance to my life

MY BEAUTIFUL
WORLD

Above all of deep

wisdom

[signature]

Know and understand

Your past, but do not dwell

on it, and you will be

master of your future

[signature]

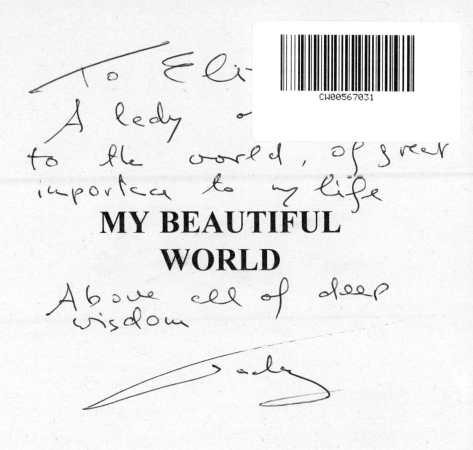

MY BEAUTIFUL WORLD

DEATH & REBIRTH

by
Tadeusz de Gromoboy

First published in Great Britain 2002
by Tadeusz de Gromoboy
76 Great Titchfield Street,
London W1P 7AF

**British Library Cataloguing-in-Publication Data.
A catalogue record for this book
is available from the British Library.**

ISBN 0 9538 743 0 3

Typeset in 10.5pt Times New Roman
By Chris Cowlin

Cover Illustration:
MEDITATION POWER
Hans Georg Leiendecker

Printed and bound in Great Britain

TABLE OF CONTENTS

INTRODUCTION

Before you is the story of an extraordinary life, but more than that as well Tadeusz de Gromoboy's life is but half over, and in another sense it is just beginning. In the telling of it, we are brought through fascinating, sometimes charmingly humorous and poignant adventures to the founding of what may become one of Brazil's greatest and most lasting contributions to the human spirit: Instituto Atalanta.

Though it has been through Tadeusz and his life's partner Elizabeth that Atalanta has become possible and real in Brazil, it represents at the same time far more than either of them. At the close of the twentieth century and moving into its successor we humans are at the threshold of a new era, but passage into it is perilous. We face ecological, environmental, social and spiritual crises quite capable of destroying vast portions of the human race and rendering life altogether impossible for those who would succeed us. Through disengagement from a now rapidly disintegrating and crumbling world, and through the formation of small, self-sustaining communities which are ecologically self-renewing and spiritually developed, it may be possible not just to escape the old, but to be a vital vehicle for the new. The Instituto Atalanta is the living germ of this altogether essential possibility for Brazil. And it opens up an environmental and spiritual future for the world which may soon prove to be Brazil's destiny and its special gift to the twenty-first century and beyond.

All great dreams and especially the necessary ones are dreamt by extraordinary dreamers, individuals at once both within life and yet larger than it, both grand and, like all of us, also vulnerable and even frail. Tadeusz de Gromoboy's story is one of tragedy and courage, of uncertainty and vision. In intimate partnership with his equally extraordinary wife, Elizabeth, Tadeusz's journey is in the service of an idea which may be the last and best hope for humankind in our increasingly perilous times. I invite you to take this journey with Tadeusz, for in the Instituto Atalanta, which is its destination, may be found not only many of our individual destinies, but a very deep and significant part of Brazil's destiny as well.

Stephen A. Erickson, PhD Yale University
Professor of Philosophy
and '*E. Wilson Lyon*' Professor of Humanities
(Claremont, California   USA)

ABOUT THE AUTHOR

Tadeusz Szczesny Walerian Rudolf de Gromoboy Dabrowicki was born in Krakow, Poland, on 13 January 1933. He was loved by his parents and was always a happy child, no matter what the circumstances.

During the war he was several times shot at, and suffered hunger and illnesses from which most people died. He had little schooling as a result of the war until he came to England when he was twelve years old. He graduated from the University of London in chemistry with an honours degree when he was twenty-one. He chose a lecturing career and became one of the youngest heads of department. He obtained a doctorate and post-doctoral qualifications in subjects ranging from metallurgy through linguistics to business administration. He loved teaching, but was also interested in politics, became a member of the executive of the Liberal Party and, as a hobby, directed an international student cabaret and edited a political-economic student newspaper.

He always loved life and used to dream on his way to school that everyone in his surroundings would be happy. If they needed financial help he would give it to them; nobody who was close to him would suffer, if he could help it.

A childish dream, it became reality in most unexpected ways.

He intensely believed that humanity could achieve anything it wanted to and that there would be cooperation between all nations.

He frequently spoke, and published one or two articles, about the necessity of first an economic and then a political federation of Europe, when he was still at school and later in university. He treasures an article about himself in *Senet*, the University of London newspaper, which he found when looking through his files. It reminds him that he predicted many of the events which happened in Europe thirty and forty years later regarding the unification of the continent.

He married for the first time when he was twenty-seven years old and had two sons of whom he is very proud. Soon after his second son was born in 1966 he developed a non-malignant cancerous growth, which since it covered all his intestines could not be removed by operation. He was opened and closed again. He was kept under opium until he decided to defend his doctoral thesis in metallurgy, which he had written before his illness. He stopped taking opium, had his viva, i.e. defended his thesis, in hospital.

His growth vanished and he went straight from hospital to his college to deliver a lecture. He felt his students needed it since it was the last before their final examination.

In 1970 he decided to make some money. He designed and built 64 flats and houses, and was chairman of three companies whilst continuing his work in the university. He did become wealthy, but lost nearly all he had in 1974 after an accident when a drunk driver ran over him.

He used to consider himself the "happiest man in the world". After the accident he decided he had been wrong. The "happiest person in the world" is the person he is now!

This is where the book starts.

DEDICATION

This book is dedicated to Elizabeth Malvina Restaino, the best wife in the world, at least for me. Without her understanding of what was happening to me and her knowledge which goes beyond the logical, it would have taken me much longer to come to the point which enabled me to write this book.

I also want to thank Mucke, known to others as Karin Preis, whose attitude to life contributed greatly to the many changes which occurred in my life. She was my first girlfriend; I met her when I was five years old and she is still my best friend.

Finally I want to thank Lilian Restaino who has something very special in her which I am sure helped me on my path, and I am equally sure will help many others on their path.

The whole Restaino family is one that I admire and one that has tremendous potential. I am grateful to all of them, particularly Antonio, the head of the family, for having accepted me as part of them and therefore contributing to the work I know I have to do.

My first wife, Barbara, with her down-to-earth attitude and courage in expressing her feelings, has been of great value to my evolution. She too, therefore, deserves my deep gratitude.

David Lindsay, in London, deciphered my difficult handwriting, gave me much encouragement and typed most of the manuscript. Maria Silvia Affonso did the same with the last three chapters which I wrote after returning to Brazil. Many thanks to them.

Sao Paulo, 6th December 1995

POSTSCRIPT DEDICATION

After finishing *My Beautiful World* I realised that once I had embarked on the path of creating the "Instituto Atalanta", even when it was still only in my mind, I had frequently not behaved in a normal and composed manner. I often experienced pressure in my chest area and spoke in a manner and voice which, so my wife told me, did not sound like my usual self.

Invariably when this happened, no matter in what part of the world we were, Ivani Gracia in Sao Paulo knew about it and prayed for me in her own fashion. In her opinion, there are forces which do not like what I am doing and try to stop or destroy me. Even semi-strangers and close relatives, who are normally very pleasant to me, for inexplicable reasons sometimes act in ways which cause me moral and physical pain. Ivani, who is a spiritist, and said she went through similar experiences when she started her own work, not only knows whenever this happens but does her best to protect me. At first I found it difficult to acknowledge her interpretation of my difficulties. I am, however, still a scientist and must accept facts, particularly if they are reproducible. I thank her and her group for protecting me in the way they do, and am now learning to do this in my own way.

I must mention Andrea Francez, a lawyer in Sao Paulo, whose help in promoting the idea of "Atalanta" has been completely selfless. Until recently I did not realise how deeply she felt the importance of "Atalanta". She also suggested that she would attend to the publication of *My Beautiful World* in Brazil. She gives her time freely and can always be relied upon. I also want to thank my sons who read the manuscript and, just before we left England in April 1996, made several comments most of which I incorporated.

My first grandson, Joshua, was born on 4th February 1996. I want to dedicate this book to him as well, not only because he is a grandson whom I love, but also because he represents new life.

Sao Paulo, 7th May 1996

FOREWORD

This book was suggested to me by friends and mediums, and finally became my own desire. I started writing it before the last events described in it happened.

After I wrote it, I realised that I had done so on two levels: one I hope an interesting story starting with my near death, practically miraculous cure and glorious love experiences, leading in a most unusual way to meeting the woman who was to become my wife, the best wife on this earth, followed by metaphysical experiences and a complete change of my life path. The other, the implication of these experiences, and what I like to think of as the elevation of my spirit, or perhaps its remembering what it intended to do or just bringing this to my conscious memory.

The book shows how an orthodox scientist evolves into a spiritual person, prepared to accept that there are many aspects of life which cannot be explained by 'science' as understood by the average person.

It describes various interesting phenomena which cannot at present be explained, yet are facts. These include voices emerging from mediums, some of them stating that they come from people who have died; voices appearing on audio tapes which were not heard by people making the recordings; voices claiming to be those of "spirits" coming out of radio receivers; computers "conversing" with their controllers; and psychic surgery also known as bloodless surgery. It shows how I began to know various things which I could not know because I had no conscious knowledge of them, such as the effect of ordinary electromagnetic waves on living cells, or because they had not yet happened but did happen whilst I was writing this book.

It tries to show how our top scientists have also demonstrated phenomena which are "impossible" scientifically and how many people simply block knowledge which to them is uncomfortable.

Dramatic changes which are occurring in this world are discussed; certain individuals, and very recently I myself, have been forecasting them, some by scientific means and others by "intuition", or was it from tapping into the All-Pervasive Energy?

It also shows how many of us feel that we ought to react to the present-day happenings and what the probable near future is going to be.

It ends with the formation of an Institute, which I had thought about consciously, but the details of which had been shown me by the All-Pervasive Energy.

CHAPTER 1

The New Beginning
World you are beautiful.

All we have to do is suspend our doubts and distractions, believe and be prepared to sacrifice for this belief what we know has to be sacrificed.

On 11th January 1974 I visited my parents in the evening. They lived only ten minutes of fast walking from our house, but I used the car. At 11pm I left their flat and crossed the road to where my car, a sports Audi which I had bought a year earlier and absolutely loved, was parked at the roadside. It stood between two other parked cars. As I was about to open the driver's door, I noticed another car, driving close to all the other parked cars, rapidly accelerating. There was no time to run the three steps along my car to the pavement. All I could do was jump onto the bonnet of the accelerating car and hold onto its aerial. It braked hard, then backed so that I slid off the bonnet onto the road surface and then drove forward again. First the front then the back wheels went over my hips, my face pointing towards the pavement and downwards. What I felt I did not afterwards remember. Another car stopped; the driver left his wife to look after me and prevent other cars running over me, while a pedestrian ran to the telephone to call an ambulance and the police. The helpful driver then chased the hit and run driver, caught and stopped him, and asked him to wait for the police; he took a note of his car number and tried to remember his bearded face. Suddenly, the bearded man reversed and drove off at high speed.

I was taken to the Hammersmith Hospital, one of London's major teaching hospitals. There Dr Galasco was called, their top orthopaedic surgeon, since apart from a scarred right cheek and forehead, my head seemed all right with no bones broken and my main obvious injuries were to the back and hip, some eighteen fractures and cracks. Just before he arrived I died, clinically. Resuscitation worked, but Galasco knew he had

1

to mend my body as best he could in a very limited time. Anaesthetics could not be administered for I could have died again. If I should wake up during the operation the shock might kill me. He had no choice but to put, as best he could, my bones into the right position without cutting me open. Fortunately, he was a highly-skilled professional.

Days later I woke up, pulled the oxygen mask off my face and whispered loudly, "A cigarette, a cigarette." A kind visitor of another patient took out a packet of cigarettes and was about to light one, with the oxygen hissing out of my discarded mask. A nurse looked up and screamed. An explosion was avoided. I fell back into my comfortable coma.

Some time later I saw my left leg high in the air and my mother-in-law lying in a bed next to mine. Was this reality or imagination? I could not decide. I called out. The person in the bed beside me was an elderly man, not my mother-in-law. All very confusing. I returned to my other world, where there was peace and no confusion.

Days later I opened my eyes again. There were distinctly nurses in the room and from the side of my eyes I could see other beds. There was a mask on my face. I tried to move. One leg was in the air and the other would not respond, but one arm did. I took my mask off and moved my head from side to side. I was in a large hospital ward with eighteen or twenty other patients. Why was I here? Obviously my legs, probably my back, were injured. But why? My hand went to my face. My cheek felt peculiar, probably stitched. My forehead felt different. I called a nurse.

"Why am I here? What is wrong with me?"

"You will be all right. You are being well looked after."

"But what happened? What is wrong with me?"

"I don't know what happened, a car accident, I think. Your leg and hips are broken so do not try to move. You will soon be all right. I shall call a doctor."

I closed my eyes. When I opened them a young doctor asked how I felt. How does one feel when only one arm moves? A little annoyed, a little confused, but not frightened. Somehow I shall move the rest of my body.

"Tell me exactly what is wrong with me."

"Your left femur head is broken. Your hips are broken. Your back is injured. At present you may not have much feeling in parts of your body, but you will soon be all right. Our senior consultant is looking after you."

"My face?"

"Oh, just minor cuts, nothing broken."

"What happened?"

I did not hear the answer. I was asleep again.

Funny, twenty-one years later, I remember all these details. A few years ago I did not. Perhaps the reason is that now I realise that God comes through our wounds, through our vulnerability; that I am not a victim of my accident; that I created it myself; that it was a call for ending my habit of a life which I did not want to continue, and that I therefore subconsciously asked for this or another major accident.

When my mind cleared again - no perhaps it was always clear - but when my conscious mind perceived the outside world again, I relaxed and tried to take in my surroundings. Simple: a ward in an old hospital, somebody moaning, somebody snoring, somebody shouting, one bed with screens around it, someone about to die? No, I am not going to stay here. Oh, but I cannot walk. I seem to be tied down to my bed. So call a nurse, a doctor, and get out of here. I am young; I am going to get well but not in this atmosphere of suffering and death. Young? How old am I? Who am I? I have a family, two young sons, parents who love me and an attractive wife who loves me as well. I certainly love her. What do I do when I am not in a hospital? I think I teach, no, lecture in a college. What college? Somewhere in the University of London. A picture of Senate House is in front of me. But what College? What subject? No, that is too difficult. I shall sleep a little, then I shall know.

I open my eyes again. My wife and my mother-in-law are standing next to me. The confusion clears. They tell me where I am and that a car ran over me. I insist that I want to get out of this room with all the sick people around me. I want to be taken to a single room. I am insured for private treatment. It seems to me that I can now think clearly.

The next day my bed, with me and all the wires, weights and screws that go through me, is gently rolled into a private room. Why do I want to sleep again? I have to stay awake and exercise my arm; it is my right arm, the most important arm. The rest will move later.

When I wake up, I am alone. On my left is a window and just outside it is a grey wall - no sky, no grass, no trees. I want to see them! At my side is a bell attached to the bed. I press it. A nurse comes. I am thirsty and hungry. A cup of tea and some toast arrive. Then a doctor. Can I smoke and drink? "Yes." Good. There is a telephone on my right side for which I have asked. I ring my wife; she is pleased that I am conscious. I ask for a bottle of whisky and some cigarettes.

Doctors come every day, X-ray equipment is wheeled into the room every few days and blood tests are taken nearly every day. I reach for my bottle of whisky frequently, pour a good measure into a glass, drink it and smoke. When the bottle is empty, my wife brings a new one. She also brought a small television. Visitors come frequently, but I cannot see the sky, the grass or the trees; only a grey wall is outside the window.

One day some colleagues from my college asked me whether I could write the examination papers which I have always written. Of course, with pleasure, but I will have to dictate them because writing is still difficult for me. When I start dictating I realise that I remember the outline of much that I lectured on, but not the mathematical details. It was quite a shock as I considered myself a very competent lecturer in my field, and believed myself to be liked by my students. I certainly loved lecturing. Some days later, a nurse asked me what languages I spoke and whether I could translate something for her. I seemed to have been speaking in a multitude of languages whilst I was in a coma. "Certainly," I said. But I could not. I had lost some of my languages. Nothing to worry about, I shall be a student again and re-learn the mathematical aspects of chemistry and metallurgy which I seem to have forgotten, and later the languages. First, I have to see the sky and the grass.

Helga Reed, a friend of mine and an ex-nurse, came to visit me. I complained bitterly that I could not see the sky and the grass. It had become an obsession. "I shall get you the sky and the grass - just wait a few minutes."

She went out and came back with a nurse. Together they wheeled me out onto the balcony, with all the bits of iron to which I was screwed. I can see sky and grass. Tears flow down my cheeks. The world is beautiful. I shall be grateful to her all my life for having shown me again what I needed. At that time I had no idea why there was this obsession with the sky and the green grass. Now that I can see auras round trees, feel some energies of nature and do not care whether people think I am crazy, I

4

understand the absolute necessity to communicate with nature.

A few days later I was "unscrewed". One pin had to be taken out from my bone. The consultant arrived with several student doctors. I had by then become quite a celebrity because my injuries were such that they did not think I would survive. He asked whether I wanted a local anaesthetic, preferring that I did not because he wanted to show the students that it could be done fairly painlessly. It was not painless; I must have paled a little, but continued smiling. He ushered the students out, said thank you and quickly gave me a pain-killing injection.

I had started lifting small sandbags with my good arm a few days earlier, and was now taken down for physiotherapy every day. I could soon move both arms equally well and later even one leg slightly. I could certainly put my weight on it. Since some nerves were torn out of my backbone and with the left sciatic severed in my hip, it was obvious to the medical profession that I would have problems.

I refused to accept this. I knew I would walk and think normally again. I started to write and telephone all over the world, asking friends whether they knew some way or somebody who could help me. Since I was still in the room with only a grey wall outside the window and was being wheeled, in a wheelchair by now, once a day to physiotherapy where again I could not see the sky and grass, I made arrangements to be transferred to another, smaller, orthopaedic hospital outside London. Galasco was a superb surgeon, a good person, but he could do no more for me. I wanted much more physiotherapy and above all a room on the ground floor where I could be permitted to wheel myself, and later go on crutches, out into the open. I began to realise that much of the work required to heal my body I would have to do myself.

The atmosphere in Hillington Hospital was superb. I learned to walk on crutches, and to go up and down three stairs in the therapy room. Since the physiotherapists realised they had a slightly crazy person on their hands, they brought pieces of equipment into my room after the physio-therapy section closed, so that I could continue my training in the evenings and on Sundays.

One night I woke up uncertain where I was. I had no major brain injury, so I decided to put it down to confusion resulting from exhaustion.

After my release, one leg still useless, I returned home. This proved a traumatic experience, since I could not manage our stairs for some time and did not seem to be able to remember what our bedroom looked like. Everything was a little confusing. Marius, my eight-year-old younger son, sometimes took me out to the park in my wheelchair and pretended it was a racing car. We had great fun, though at times I thought I would fly out of my chair. Soon I stopped using the chair and learned to drive my car again, using a stick to depress the clutch. This was of course ridiculous, so with great sadness I sold my, to me glorious, sports car and bought a small automatic. Then I was informed that my driving licence was no longer valid, since I had suffered brain injury, and that I would have to be examined again, or get a suitable medical certificate. So I was examined. I had to drive very carefully since my reactions were poor and I could only drive slowly, but I could not drive so slowly that the examiner would notice that my reactions were not what they ought to be. My driving licence was returned.

I drove myself every day to the physiotherapy department of my first hospital in the hope that they could do something more for me, but soon realised that they had reached their limit.

During one of my visits there, I became confused again and asked one of the nurses what had happened to my class. I knew I had to deliver a lecture, but could not find my students. This caused a slight panic. The psychiatrist was called and then the neurologist; electrodes were put on my head and I saw flashing lights - an electro-encephalography was in progress. By that time, I knew exactly where I was. I knew I was not crazy, but was interested in what caused those lapses of memory and states of confusion. The examination showed nothing. The neurological consultant became a friend and took me on his motorcycle on a round of pubs in the city. That all this had a purpose and that I was running away from my past life, I did not know at that time. But I knew that I was going to be well, an absolute conviction.

I knew nothing about complementary healing since I was an orthodox scientist. But my previous enquiries started paying off -, a friend had a Chinese doctor staying with her, who had come to England to learn English. He suggested that he could try acupuncture. I had never heard of acupuncture before. After a short time I began to move my toes. The "impossible" was happening. I had some internal problems and was bleeding through my anus; this too cleared up. Then a Swiss friend suggested that I go to an alternative sanatorium, Friedborn Sanatorium, near Bad-Sackingen on the German-Swiss border. "Miracles happen there," she said. Since "miracles" was the only thing left to me, I went. The daughter of the owners, Brigitte Greim, received me and examined me together with their resident doctor. Yes, I would walk normally again, they were certain. I would take my first steps without a stick four weeks after they started work on me. But I would have to do everything they said. After I had learned to curl my toes as a result of acupuncture I was prepared to believe that anything was possible. After all I had started out on my quest by saying anything I wanted to happen could happen. All we have to do is believe and suspend our doubts. Though, at the time, my belief was still that there is something purely physical to the "alternative" methods. Brigitte and the doctor thought the same. Neither they nor I believed in, or had indeed heard much about, "spiritual healing". They simply had a different methodology. A clean body together with a willing mind and a healthy diet was, in their opinion, the foundation of all healing. They started with a complete fast for three weeks - herb tea, water in which potatoes, cabbage and some other vegetables had been boiled and then removed, some natural vitamins and a little fruit juice.

Every morning there were yoga exercises modified by Brigitte. Her commentary during these exercises implied that if you believed in what they were meant to heal, they would do so. Those who could, had to walk through forests and meadows; those who could not, had to appreciate the vegetation and the sky, and imagine they were doing exercises and walking.

She spoke of the healing energy of running water and prana. Yet when years later I realised that she was a healer, or what is known in England as spiritual healer, she found it difficult to accept it, and did not want to have anything to do with it. This in spite of knowing that she could, by massaging patients, achieve what no other masseuse achieved. An interesting example of a person of great ability and knowledge being unable to accept what they do, and know that they can do. But at that time even I had not heard of spiritual healing.

On the seventh day my behind was literally burned, so that an enormous blister formed. The liquid from the blister was taken out and injected back into me. Nobody could explain how this worked, except that they knew from experience that it would heal and repair my body. A whole range of massages and water treatments were performed on me. When I started eating it was purely vegetarian, and mostly raw food.

On the first day of the fifth week I got out of my bed, and for the first time in a year walked on my own two legs, without even a stick. I had a shower, and walked past the lift and down the stairs to the dining room. My legs shook and I was covered in sweat, but I had walked on my own. I am a scientist; I may not understand, but I have to accept facts. It is sad that there are many who can see facts, but if they are not reproducible at will they reject them as unscientific, and often a few months later will even say that they did not observe the facts which they found unacceptable.

Brigitte did introduce me to Zen Buddhism. I read a book, but did not really understand much. I saw, however, several people cured, even of cancer, after they had left orthodox hospitals declared as incurable, and realised that there is more to life than orthodox science has to offer. By their conviction of being able to cure people, Brigitte and her parents, so I began to feel at the time, achieved results. I did not quite understand how. She, her parents who started the sanatorium, and the staff there were all convinced that it was the fasting, diet, massage, yoga, fresh air, etc., that were responsible for their incredible results. I could not get rid of a niggling feeling that what they were doing was correct, and responsible for much of the healing, yet that there was something more to it. At first I thought that they instilled in their patients a will to get better. That too was certainly true. But I began to wonder whether this conviction of being able to heal, and the deep feeling of "love" one experienced there, was not the cause of something more. It was the beginning for me. I did not pursue the thought at the time. Today, I know that if we believe in something it can create an atmosphere, an energy which seems to be visible to some. This energy can cause things we desire to happen. If you ask for proof of this energy and for an instrument to show the existence and intensity of this energy before you are prepared to accept it, then pause and think. Do you ask for an instrument which registers your dreams before you are prepared to believe that you have dreamt? If you suddenly think of somebody, the telephone rings and that person is on the phone, do you not believe that you thought of that person before he rang? If you feel somebody is staring at you from behind, you turn and find yourself looking straight into their eyes, do you not believe what you felt a moment ago? If you do, then you must accept that there are energies which are not yet measurable. We all exude energies, some healing and some hurting. Brigitte's and her parents' were healing energies, and just as the warmth radiated from one body will cause another body to become warm, so they affected their staff, and they too were able to heal.

After eight weeks, I drove back to London, with my crutches in the boot and my stick on the back seat. On uneven ground I sometimes had to use it. Even today, when I think back to that journey, tears of joy flow down my cheeks.

I had learned that most things, certainly not all, that you want and believe in are possible. Those which are not would be wrong for you, as was proved to me very clearly during the next phase of my life.

I stayed on a vegetarian diet for some time but did not think a great deal about what really happened in Friedborn Sanatorium. I still had much to fight for. My memory was still poor. I could not remember south London, even parts to which I had been going frequently. Some of my scientific knowledge had gone; the year before the accident was practically non-existent in my conscious memory and many friends I did not remember. I went to Imperial College, but this time as a student and attended all those lectures which I used to give. It was very hard going as mathematical aspects of science did not want to stay in my memory. I could have lectured but only with notes, and I had never taken notes into a lecture room before. I believed in looking at the students whilst lecturing. I could then feel when I lost them and repeat what I had been trying to get over, in a different way.

During my prolonged hospitalisation, all three companies which I had formed collapsed. My finances were poor, but we still had some assets left in the form of one or two flats and houses which we had refurbished but on which there were bank loans. There came a moment when no cash was left. My sons were in expensive private schools.

I knew I would get reasonable compensation from the insurance company of the person who had run me over, but it could take another two years before this came through. The lecturers' union was prepared to give me a loan of a few thousand pounds, but required a guarantor, a formality. I asked a very close friend of mine to provide this guarantee. He refused. "Charity begins at home," he said or words to that effect. Somehow I managed without the loan.

It was perhaps the best lesson I had, and it helped many other people. In the future, when my finances improved again, many people asked me for loans, or if I knew they needed one I would suggest it myself. I felt good doing so, though once I thought I would never get it back. Fortunately the woman I was meant to marry, though it took me over fifty years to know who she was, has the same attitude. It gives me infinite pleasure to help. I shall always be grateful to these friends, who unwittingly made my life fuller. What is perhaps even more important, they have helped me to understand that I cannot expect everybody to react the way I do, and that an apparently negative reaction can have positive results. I like them as much as I always did, perhaps even more. They have helped me to be of service to others and realise that giving often results in a deeper pleasure than getting.

One day my bank manager telephoned. We had had many a glass of whisky together during office hours and many a lunch, and he had invited my wife and myself to one or two receptions for managers and valued clients. I had been a client since I was eighteen years old, with a slowly rising bank balance. Then when I went into business, whilst still lecturing, he managed first small and then larger loans for me and my companies. Everything was always repaid on or before time. Now it must have been obvious to him I was in difficulties.

"How are you? I have not seen you for a long time."

"Oh, much better. I can walk. There are still some difficulties, but I shall overcome them," I answered with a firm voice but shaking inside.

What if he wants me to sell my remaining assets now, to repay quickly the outstanding loans to my various companies? Some of the assets were not ready for sale. If I have to sell now, nothing will be left; perhaps even the outstanding loans will not be covered.

"If I send a car for you, do you think you can come for lunch?"

I did not understand. He was a busy man and I was no longer a valuable client; there was no need to tell me over lunch that all my loans had to be repaid now. He could send me a letter or, if he wanted to be very polite, ask me to his office.

"What would you like to eat? They have a variety of restaurants at the West London Hilton."

I knew they were all fairly expensive. What was the meaning of this?

"Your company will be good enough; any food that will go with it will be a bonus. Whatever you prefer I shall enjoy."

"How about Japanese? I hear you have been on a diet, eating healthy, tasteless food. I thought you would enjoy a change, if you think your constitution will take it."

I understood even less. I had not won the pools. I did not even play them.

"That is very nice of you. Yes, Japanese. I shall be delighted."

"I shall collect you in fifteen minutes."

I knew miracles had happened with my health, but what miracle was this? My hands were shaking. They had not done so for a long time.

Music was playing in the background; a pot was boiling in the middle of the table, and a bottle of good wine stood next to us.

"I have known you for a long time. Your assets are good, if you do not lose your head. Accident or no accident, I know you will not, even if I have to try to manage a small additional loan for you." For the first time in my life a tear rolled down my cheek during a business lunch.   "It must be God who is looking after me," was the only thought I had.

Everything else was blurred. "Yes, I shall be the happiest person on earth again, I don't know how, I don't know when, but I shall."

Twenty years later, I do not know whether I am the happiest person, but I do not know anybody who is happier, in spite of a funny leg, a bit of kidney missing and open heart surgery. I have learned that in my case and generally, perhaps not always, believing in something intensely usually causes it to be so.

I decided to take a degree in a different field to prove to myself that I was not a complete moron. My IQ had gone up from 99, average, to 136 nine months after the accident. I knew that the average PhD was under 130, but I felt inadequate and knew that I should not work in pure science again. I decided on Business Administration on an international level. The London School of Business would not have me. IMEDE, part of the University of Lausanne, seemed to me more appropriate anyway. I applied and was accepted at a level higher than I had aimed for, since I had no degree in business administration and no experience to speak of in this field.

Before the course, due to start in January 1977, I went to Friedborn Sanatorium again because my leg was giving me trouble. On my way back a message reached me via relatives where I was going to spend a night, that my father had had a heart attack whilst on holiday in Austria. He was taken to the university clinic in Graz, whilst my mother, who had had a coronary two years before, was advised to remain in the hotel in which they had been, some sixty miles from Graz. I turned the car round and drove back across the Alps continuously for some ten hours. When I arrived in Graz, I could no longer see clearly, so I went to a police station on the outskirts and explained that I did not want to cause an accident. Could they help? Without any hesitation, they asked me to follow one of their cars which piloted me to the hospital. After two weeks' driving daily between mother's hotel and father in hospital, I was exhausted. Father was better - he would live. I brought mother to a hotel near the rehabilitation sanatorium to which father was sent and drove home.

When I arrived back in London in the late evening, my wife greeted me, but there was something wrong. The next morning, after I hugged my two sons and they had gone to school, she said, "I have met somebody else. What are you going to do about it?"

In a way, it was like a bolt of lightning from a blue sky; in a way, it seemed a good thing. I was not hurt and not worried. Why? I did love her and thought our life had been a good one. "Why? Were we not happy together? Had we not come closer to each other after my accident?" I asked.

"Not really. I need somebody with whom I want to be and start a new life. You can keep the children."

I knew what my reaction should be and knew what it was. At the time, I did not understand why it was or what it was.

"Who is the gentleman in question?"

"You do not know him. It does not matter."

"To me it matters, because obviously our sons are going to see you and I would like to know in what company they will then be."

"It is too early now. You can meet him later," she answered.

12

Chapter 1

Instinct told me there was something wrong but I let it go. I was not at the level at which I am now. Anyway, I wanted my wife to be happy.

"There is a flat we have just finished refurbishing. Take it and move in there with your friend. The children and I shall manage."

I was in shock, but not worried. I had an idea of cooking and enjoyed doing it. My sons, to me the most important people in my life, were going to stay with me; that was all that mattered. I had no job; my health was not perfect and my memory was poor. I should have despaired, yet somehow I knew that what was happening was right for me.

On the next day, a reaction set in and I cried for much of the day. In the afternoon a friend, whose wife had also met someone else, came and saw me in this sorrowful state. When I explained what had happened he said, "Go have a bath, shave and come to my house. I shall have two charming ladies visiting me."

When I arrived I realised that he was interested in one of the ladies, but it was the other, her younger sister, Morena, a girl about my height with a superb figure and beautiful flowing long hair, who struck me. My mood changed instantaneously. This sort of thing did not happen to me normally. It was not overpowering but pleasant. A chord had been struck which resonated in me, a term frequently used, but how many of us think more deeply about its significance? A chord or a sound wave was emitted. Do we emit waves? She was twenty years younger and had just left university. I came the next day to my friend, where I knew she was going to spend a few days, with a bunch of roses and asked her out to dinner. She was not an "easy" girl - I do not like them - and there was something very lovely about her. She did not flatter me, but I knew she appreciated me. We started going out regularly. She helped me tremendously in getting over the shock of my marriage splitting up, at a moment when I had not yet fully recovered from my own accident and the near death of my father. I was happy. I had my sons at home; they were the most important people to me. My love for them had always been perhaps too great, for it made me very vulnerable, as I was to realise in the near future.

Before Christmas 1976, my wife telephoned.

"We have decided we should go back to our previous partners. You have guests at home now. May I come tomorrow?"

"Of course, we shall discuss it personally then."

13

I was confused and had a peculiar feeling in my gut. For our sons' sake, should we come together again? Obviously my personality had not been the right one for her if, even when I was in great need of moral support, she had decided to have a romance with someone else and had, as I was told later, brought books on divorce to our home whilst I was still in hospital. I had not minded her leaving me. If I was not the right person then why should she spoil her life? I was only 43; she was 37 years old. Even then I must have realised that convenience can numb the soul; that without a synergetic relationship one could not lead a fruitful life; the children would feel the wrong energies, and the negative effect on them would outweigh the beauty of having two parents in the house. No, only if we could really love and trust each other would I be prepared to continue with our marriage. I did not know then, but felt instinctively, what I know now. If the energies in a family are not harmonious, whatever the outside appearance, all in the household suffer, become bitter, corrupt or aggressive. Nothing, however, is completely predetermined; there are only greater or smaller probabilities. Our free will can change these probabilities for better or worse. So when my wife came on the next day I said, "Let's try to fall in love with each other again. Let us see each other from time to time at first; then if we feel like it, more frequently and then, if we both feel that we can have the very special relationship that a good marriage requires, we can come together again."

"But you promised I could come back. If you wish I shall not see him again."

I then understood what my gut feeling had probably meant. Both felt they owed it to their children, rather than their previous partners, when they decided to go back to their original marriage partner. Both would either continue to see each other or think constantly of what they were missing. I may not have been a perfect husband, but I intended to be one in future, on a reciprocal basis. "No, I only promised that we would talk about it," I answered. "Let us be fair to each other and make sure that we fully understand and love each other, and do not make mistakes again. For our and our children's sake."

"No, I do not want it that way. You promised I could come back. If you do not want me now, then I shall go."

And she went.

In a way I felt relieved. Now I knew I sensed that there was something else meant for me in my future - something more important, more beautiful, waiting for me. Now I know what it was. Now I frequently have such feelings and experience has taught me to accept them.

One day I suggested to Morena that we go to a hotel out in the country together. To my delight she agreed. We had a delicious dinner and felt completely at ease with each other. When we retired to our room I had a shower first, went to bed and waited for her. She had forgotten her dressing gown. When the door from the bathroom opened, a tall slim girl appeared with my dressing gown thrown around her but not closed. Long flowing black hair framed her face and touched her breasts. They were very large, but beautifully formed. Below was a wonderfully shaped body, a dream of womanhood. With a gentle smile she approached the bed and took off completely the dressing gown.

"Am I all right?"

Nobody could wish for anything better. She lay down on the other bed. I came to her.

Soon I had a telephone call from mother telling me that father was well enough to come back home. Since mother had had a coronary infarct a short time ago and father had only just had one, neither could carry any luggage. Father was advised not to fly. So I decided to drive down to Austria and collect them. I asked Morena to help. It would be fun to be with her and certainly make the journey easier. She was a good driver, though she had never driven outside England.

I had not told my parents that my wife had left me. When we arrived and I introduced Morena, they showed no trace of astonishment.

Mother's gaze dropped down to my right hand where I used to wear my wedding ring. There was no ring there now. We had dinner. Father was already staying in the hotel where mother had been whilst he was in the convalescent centre. After dinner I asked them:

"Are you not surprised? I am here with Morena and not my wife."

"No," mother answered. "She left you, didn't she?"

"Yes," father added. "I have already explained that Morena is my niece and came to help you with the driving. I arranged for a double room for you. That's what you wanted, wasn't it?"

"Perception, guesswork, intuition?" I asked them.

Mother answered. "When you came in without your wife, I knew something was wrong. No ring on your finger and I knew she had left you. But I already knew before you arrived."

Father looked in splendid condition. Mother was better than I expected. I knew that life was going to be good again. I was happy.

The romance with my newly found girlfriend, Morena, flourished. We went to Tunisia for a holiday and soon I felt extremely happy again and became quite addicted to her.

On 6th January 1977 I left for my postgraduate business administration course in Lausanne. I worked extremely hard, some 14 hours every day. I felt I had to prove to myself and the world that my brain was still functioning.

My parents, who loved my sons as much as I did, moved into my house to look after them during my six months' absence. On 13th January I flew back to London to spend my birthday with my sons. I noticed that my older son was not quite his happy self, but thought that it was merely because he missed me, and flew back.

CHAPTER 2

Hard Work
Believe in your intuition and you will succeed.

Some three weeks later I developed what appeared to the Lausanne doctor a heart problem and flew back to London again for a full examination. The diagnosis was that I was completely exhausted. I had been working every day until midnight, or later, and getting up at 7.00 am. My eyes had black rims under them and my face deep lines, but my heart appeared to be in good condition. I could fly back provided I worked less intensely. My elder son, I noticed, seemed even more unhappy. My father, although he loved his grandchildren as much as he loved me, and it was a great if slightly dominating love, was a disciplinarian - not in the conventional sense, though he was an old fashioned gentleman in many ways and one of the few remaining "real" gentlemen. Most young people adored him, including Morena my girlfriend, and many of his pupils, for after retiring from the army, he had become a teacher. My elder son found it difficult to behave as "old people" do, for example to play the radio at reasonable rather than high volume, and began to resent my father. Or was he just missing his mother who had so recently left him and fearing that his father might not give him the attention that was his due, since he had gone on a course outside England and had a girlfriend? Or was it simply that he needed the female energy to balance him now? I was torn between remaining at home and going back to my course. A moment's reflection told me that I had to go. At that time it seemed to me that it was the only way I could learn to love and respect myself again. I could not be a good father if I did not respect myself.

My wife's temporary partner had left her. She was alone now and wanted our children to be with her. Aleksander decided to go to his mother; Marius my younger son decided to stay with me in my house, under my parents' supervision, until I returned in three months. I had retained our house of course, since initially she did not want the children, so in the divorce which took place before Aleksander returned to her, we agreed that I would pay her half the value of the house, and retain the house itself.

Aleksander's departure hurt. I wanted both my sons and was sure that I could bring them up well, but was not prepared to persuade them to stay. I shall be for ever grateful that Marius decided to stay with me. To come back to an empty house after losing my wife, health and cash reserves as a result of my accident and the divorce, would have been very hard.

The course I was attending continued to be exhausting, particularly with the additional strain of knowing that Aleksander too had left me. In spite of all this it was, in hindsight, the most satisfying part of my life until my "second life" (or should I call it "third"?) started. Not only did I prove to myself (at that time I still needed material and tangible proof) that I was capable of regaining knowledge, but it also gave me a new insight into life. It showed me, and presumably other people, my ability to get to the right results without mathematical formulae.

Most of our "examinations" consisted of being given a case history and then extrapolating it into the future. For our first test, after one term in college, we were given details of the production statistics, cost of materials, cost of labour, sale price, etc., of a given real company for several past years and the situation of the world markets, as well as the details of the character of the directors and labour unions during that time. We were expected by use of various ratios and their extrapolation, to predict what the profits, if any, of the company were going to be and show in detail how we had arrived at our result. I tried to use the mathematical techniques we were taught, but somehow found it difficult. I no longer felt comfortable using logical mathematical tools. So I stopped and started a new approach. Somehow I knew what the answer was going to be, but I had to show how I had obtained it. I used the character of the directors and the labour force, and the world situation, and prayed that my "guess" at the final result was correct. I knew if I got the answer right in this the first examination, I would manage the rest. We did not sit all together in an examination hall. We were given a case history in the evening and expected to have the answer ready the next morning. By the time I had given up my mathematical deliberations as fruitless, it was 1.00 am. The other approach took less than an hour. I was writing at a furious rate. How I knew the answer was, at that time, a mystery to me. Perhaps what I knew was completely wrong. Perhaps my way of showing how I got to it would be unacceptable. It was important to me that at least the answer should be close to the correct one. Would it be?

Thirty-six hours later I got my answer back. A paragraph of red ink at the bottom. "Congratulations, but how the devil did you come so close to the correct answer? Your approach is a most unorthodox one."

I suddenly realised that I had trusted my intuition frequently before in my life, but had persuaded myself that I had arrived at my answer by a logical thought process. However, often you just know. I realised then that many great scientists had often known the answer intuitively. What took them time was to prove to others that their answer was the correct one.

After discussion in class of the case which we had worked on, our professor asked me privately, "Tell me, did you know the answer in advance? How did you know it? You could not have arrived at it by the means you indicated."

"I think I did," I answered without hesitation. I had again persuaded myself that it was my logical brain that was responsible. But I added, "I sometimes know things very quickly. I suppose it is a knack, like some people being able to multiply long numbers by each other instantaneously."

I was showing off, I know. But was there not perhaps a lot of truth in what I said? Do we not sometimes just know without a rapid brain process? Much later I realised that I often "know" things that logically I could not possibly have known. Even later I began to "see" future events which often, not always, became a reality. But this is jumping ahead too much.

I liked this particular professor and liked most of them, but felt a particular empathy with him, so I added, "I had an accident, you see, and was told I would never think clearly again. So it is important to me to show that I can arrive at correct answers, even if I do not use orthodox means."

"Hm," he said, "I have come across something like this before. Cultivate this gift. You may get further than I did."

We never discussed it again. But I had regained my confidence completely. I knew I would do well in all the subjects. Of course I would have to continue to work hard. I knew I was no business genius, but I knew I would do well if I worked, used my own "intuitive gift" and did not trust in luck.

I also knew that in my future life what I had to do was to believe in myself, believe without any doubts in my mind, and usually the right answer would come. Provided, of course, I sought answers which would not hurt others or myself. These thoughts were just flashes to be forgotten, but to return from time to time.

During the course, I had to fly back to London again to attend the final court proceeding relating to my divorce. With hindsight, I am surprised that I felt no regrets, and had no hard feelings at that time.

CHAPTER 3

The Final Split
There are energies which many of us do not understand.

My family had finally been split, my career in the university had been terminated and my cash assets, high in past years, were zero. My whole world, as I had known it hitherto, was in turmoil. Yet I seemed happy and expectant.

Perhaps I had foresight then that this turmoil was necessary, that my life had to change and that I was about to find my real goals. I was always a happy person. Just before my accident I used to say, "I am the happiest person on earth." During the last few years before it I achieved everything I wanted. I worked hard but, as I now know, towards the wrong end.

A year before my accident I had what Dr Nixon called a coronary syndrome, all the symptoms of a coronary, without any scars on the heart at the end. I should have learned to slow down then and to review my life and its purpose. I did not heed the warning, so I had an accident and my wife left me. There is a reason for most things that occur in this life.

"Will you marry me?" I asked Morena.

"No, I love you, but no."

"Why?" I asked. "I am free. We could have a glorious future." I did not worry about the fact that my finances were not particularly good. I was certain that I would manage. Nor did I worry that Morena was twenty years younger. I considered myself young.

"I don't know, but no. I will move in with you after you return from your course in Lausanne and we shall see later."

The black rims under my eyes deepened. The course in Lausanne became no easier, but I continued to enjoy it. I did well in all the tests and felt confident that I was doing better than most, even though others had degrees in business administration and plenty of business experience in private firms or governments. Life was beautiful.

When I returned to my house in London, Marius was waiting for me and threw himself round my neck, one of the most beautiful moments of my life.

My parents were delighted that I had returned, but were shocked by my exhausted face. They moved back to their flat and Morena moved into my house. She sometimes helped Marius with his Latin homework and I helped with other subjects. We settled down to a delightful routine.

Marius, then eleven years old, usually returned from St Paul's, his school, at five o'clock or earlier. One day, five-thirty came and passed - no Marius. I telephoned the school. Someone had seen him leave at the usual time. My pulse rate increased. I rang the local hospital and the police. No news. I took a photograph of my son to the police station and explained what had happened. My description was passed to police in the area. Nobody had seen anything suspicious. I telephoned my ex-wife, as I felt that she had a right to know, and then those parents of Marius's friends whose number I had. My heart was racing.

"Has your son returned from school?"

"Yes, an hour ago. Why?"

"Marius has not, I am worried."

"Try X. He usually leaves together with Marius."

I did.

"Has X returned from school?"

"Oh, yes. They returned late because ...."

Because, because what? What had happened? The voice at the other end did not seem worried, in fact quite normal. Well, her son was back so why should she be worried?

"They went to the police..."

The police, oh God. What had happened?

"They had found £10 on the road and wanted to give it to the police."

I did not understand what this had to do with Marius not being back.

"They had to explain where they found it and Marius came to us."

Thank God he is all right. I had a bitter-sweet taste in my mouth.

"He tried to telephone you so you would not worry. We live close to the police station." I took several deep breaths to stop my hands shaking. "But your line was engaged all the time, and then there was no answer. He should be back any moment now."

Of course, I was ringing and trying to find out what had happened, and then drove to the police station.

I went out through the front door; there in the distance I could make out the hurried step of Marius. He was back. That was all that mattered. Life was beautiful. I wished Aleksander was here.

Morena was doing a postgraduate course in a local college. My parents, particularly father, liked her very much. I asked her again to marry me.

"No, I don't want to."

"Why? There must be a reason? I know you love me." I did not really know then what love was, though at the time I was sure I did.

"There is no reason. I do love you, but I do not want to marry. Not yet."

I just did not understand. I was reasonably good-looking and infinitely better with my sex than I had been with my ex-wife. We had lots of fun together. I thought I looked much younger than I was. I came from a good family. I did not understand. Not then. There was no material or psychological reason. I had just graduated from a prestigious college in a field that usually lead to well-paid positions. People told me that we looked good together. True, I sometimes forgot where I was, but this did not worry me as it would pass. It did not worry Morena either. So why?

For a few months "family" life was lovely. Then I noticed that something was worrying Marius. I asked him.

"Nothing, Dad, everything is fine."

I knew it was not.

The next day I asked again. It was a weekend. We talked for hours. I could always talk with my sons for hours. I consciously tried not to overpower them with my personality, nor with what I expected of them. I now know that I did not succeed, because my whole attitude to life was that a person who wants to get somewhere in life, who wants to lead a full and contented life, should try to get a degree, or as high a qualification as possible, or at least work hard at obtaining material knowledge. Only later did I realise that everybody, particularly children, prefer not to be pushed, not even by example, to a given form of life. If a given path is right for them, then a gentle indication is much more likely to be of value to them than a powerful, even if unstated, expectation.

After a time it emerged that Marius was missing his brother.

Fortunately for both of us I understood completely. He was an extremely sensitive child and, however rowdy at home, had a very warm heart; he never wanted to hurt anybody. It was probably then that I began to realise the importance of permitting everybody to use their own free will, unless it was very obviously a harmful decision.

I knew that my ex-wife wanted both our sons now, so I suggested that Marius join his brother for a trial time. His room would remain as it had always been for years. He could come back next week, month or year. They could both come back. I would always love them equally no matter where they were. I had paid their mother a lump sum when Aleksander decided to go to her; I no longer had another lump sum to pay, but would pay the schooling and other expenses for Marius to my ex-wife as long as he was with her.

And so Marius too left. I saw him every week. We often spent a whole day or even a weekend together. He seemed happy, and so did Aleksander. However much I missed them, that to me was the most important thing. I was beginning to learn that to give can be more pleasant than to get.

I tried again to be reinstated as a lecturer; I obviously had not quite accepted that my previous career had ended. I was asked to attend a physical examination to see how steady I was on my feet and a psychiatric one to examine my memory, and in particular my reactions to questioning by students.

Just before these examinations, I developed an intense cold. Morena told me to delay the tests because I was obviously not going to be at my best. I insisted I would manage. If I could get through the course at IMEDE I could do anything. Now I know that subconsciously I tried to sabotage myself.

The physical examination showed that I could not really use my legs. The fact that I could walk unaided for a short distance seemed immaterial. I suppose theoretically I was unable to walk.

The psychiatric examination also showed that my memory was erratic. I said that I was interested in politics, and yet I could not remember the names of many of the recent prominent politicians. After being told a story, I could not remember many of its details. I was obviously not the right person to deliver lectures. It hit me hard, but just for a day. I was officially retired on health grounds on a 25% pension since I had been a lecturer for only eighteen years.

I gave business advice to friends; at times, perhaps even usually, it was very good. They showed their appreciation appropriately. Sometimes it involved assessing a situation in other countries to which I had to travel. This I thoroughly enjoyed. I did not dare to take an official appointment, or act as an independent consultant, since I knew that I sometimes had short episodes of confusion, and always suggested to my friends that they take a second opinion. This stopped completely only when I knew what my future work had to be, many years later.

Morena and I travelled a lot by car in England and abroad, and on package deals. I met her parents who thought that my main reason for being with Morena was that I wanted a young woman to look after me. They were obviously opposed to our relationship, particularly her father. It hurt because I did not think I needed anybody for the physical help she could provide. I knew I would always be able to look after myself, but wanted a companion whom I could love and trust.

In the autumn of 1978 my father's school friend Richard de Bloch and his wife, who had been living in Brazil, visited them. They did so every few years. It was their wedding anniversary. I arranged a small reception for them at the Polish Air Force Club in London. I liked the atmosphere and food there. Richard's wife Cysinka asked whether she could invite a Brazilian friend who was studying at Cambridge.

"Of course," I said. "Tell her she can spend a night or two in my house."

The friend turned out to be Elizabeth, a young lady some 26 years old and an ex-student of Cysinka. When she arrived I saw a charming and well-behaved lady who walked with a limp. She had lost her wallet with her papers and all her money. I helped her to look for it; took her to the police station, and found it in the end with nothing missing, at the Baker Street Lost Property Office. No gong struck. I did not know that the second and more important part of my life had started.

Life with Morena continued to be beautiful, but she still did not want to marry me. I began to find it hard to live with a woman who, although I loved her, did not trust me sufficiently to be prepared to marry me. At least I thought at the time that it was a lack of trust. I did not know then that people sometimes do or do not do something, not knowing consciously why, and that there are deeper forces than those which we consciously recognise.

In 1978 father began to have difficulties in passing water. Examination in Charing Cross Hospital, one of London's largest and at that time most modern hospitals, including a private examination by Mr Pillips, considered an outstanding urologist, showed nothing wrong. Yet the symptoms were intense. I took him to another specialist who again could at first find nothing wrong, but had the sense to accept the fact that the symptoms existed. The only way he could think of investigating further was to operate. After the operation had been performed the surgeon went to another hospital. Nobody was prepared to tell me what had been found. I did not expect anything dramatic. I knew others who had had prostate operations. After father woke up he was perfectly happy and I brought mother home and visited my ex-mother-in-law. From there I traced the surgeon by phone.

"What did you find and what had or still has to be done?" I asked.

"It is a cancerous growth," he answered.

"What type of growth? Completely removed, I hope?"

"Well, it appears to be malignant."

The light seemed to dim around me. Father had always looked younger than he was and was very fit. The word cancer shook me.

"What now? Will you tell him or do I?"

"Of course I shall. I am afraid he will have to undergo radiotherapy to make certain it does not spread."

After I brought father back home, I took him regularly for a few weeks for radiotherapy treatment.

He described to me precisely what they were doing and asked me why. He had been teaching physics before his retirement. Of course he knew what they were doing and why.

I then realised that he had simply switched off. He did not want to accept the knowledge of his illness. Consciously he did not know what was wrong with him. I did not in my explanations use the word cancer and left everything rather vague.

I came across this switching off again eleven years later when my new mother-in-law died of cancer. After her death her husband asked, "What did she die of?"

"Cancer, father," his son answered.

"Why didn't anybody tell me?"

"But we did three months ago when the diagnosis was confirmed."

"No, I do not remember anything."

Many times in my later life I noticed this phenomenon. Perfectly intelligent people switched out of their conscious mind what was inconvenient for them. They knew, but chose for reasons they themselves may not have realised, not to know.

Right now, whilst writing the above I have made the connection between these phenomena and myself. I chose to forget much of my higher mathematics to give myself a reason not to continue my previous work. I chose to forget some of my languages and the ability to re-learn them quickly, because working as a linguist was not right for me either.

I remember well an evening at home when a Spanish film with English subtitles was shown on television. After a few sentences I realised I did not read the subtitles but understood the Spanish. Tears rolled down my cheeks. My memory had come back!

The film finished. Next day I took a Spanish book. Nothing! I understood a few words - that was all. This pattern repeated itself once or twice a year.

A psychiatrist from Cambridge and a neurologist from London met and tested me every week for some five months to find the cause of this "not quite loss" of languages and higher mathematics. They came to no conclusion. Is the brain like a computer where all knowledge is stored and all we have to do is to learn to use the access key? Was my access key damaged? How much knowledge do we have? Only what we learned during our life or is some stored genetically? A baby sucks its mother's breast, as do animals, but nobody teaches them. Some of us speak languages when under the influence of an anaesthetic. At times this can be traced to our hearing the language when a baby, but sometimes it is a language that the baby could not possibly have heard. Sometimes it is a language which nobody understands yet it sounds as though it has a well-defined structure. An ancient lost language? At the age of eight, whilst in a bathroom, I started speaking a language which I did and do not understand. I still frequently speak it because I feel I have to.

Some musicians start composing when they are small children and some children write poetry before they have learned to write essays. Is it just a genetic memory? Or is there knowledge outside our body which we can tune into. Not long ago radio waves into which we can now tune with a simple radio would have seemed phantasy. Are we certain that there are no waves into which our complex brain can tune? Or perhaps there is even more to it. Perhaps we are not only flesh whose genes remember previous life experiences, but also a spirit who remembers too.

When father's course of radiotherapy was completed, I took him to Friedborn Sanatorium where I had been literally put on my feet, and where I had met people who were told that they had cancer and then seen them leave without it. Father was not one of the lucky ones. They said they would do their best, but doubted whether they could cure him. It was the first time that I experienced doubt in Friedborn. I left him there, only to be phoned some two weeks later and told that they did not think they could do anything for him. I flew to Basel; they brought him to the airport, and I took him back to a London hospital. He deteriorated, but still did not accept that he had cancer which was rapidly spreading.

Mother decided that she wanted to take him home. A hypnotist, who was also a healer as I found out later, whom I had met when I had problems after my accident and was trying "everything", came to see father. Father said that when he touched the lower part of his body he felt as though a current passed through him. Though at that time I knew nothing about "healing" or "spiritual healing" as it is commonly called, when father asked me to touch him it made him feel much better. For a time I spent eighteen hours a day sitting next to him and stayed in my parents' flat for twenty-four hours a day. He seemed content, but was obviously passing away. At a certain stage I went home as I felt I was about to collapse and had no energy left. Once home I fell asleep immediately. After a few hours his nurse rang, saying that he would probably die any moment now. In minutes I was at his bedside and just in time to see him take his last breath.

I learned later that when a person is ready to die, and somebody he loves holds his hand, he finds it more difficult to let go. I now feel that it is wrong to hold someone whose time to go has come. I felt no sorrow, just relief for his sake. It was more difficult for mother, though she too knew that death was not the finality some seem to think it is. She was simply sorry to be separated, even if temporarily, from somebody she deeply loved.

It was April 1979, spring and a new era. Father's influence on me would remain to an extent for ever. Yet the immediate pressure of someone I loved deeply, and who loved me as much, but expected me to do many of the things he did not do and to achieve a fame which circumstances did not permit him to reach, was gone.

I had always admired my parents and felt that they were the best one could wish for. They had given me two qualities: my mother a loving spirituality, and my father an earthly ambition. Without mother I would perhaps not care so much for others and without father I would not have obtained as many degrees, and later, even if for a short period, worldly riches. Only fifteen years later did I realise that I had permitted their influence to be too overwhelming; that I could not develop to a higher level without rejecting this overwhelming power which they unwittingly exerted over me. Father expected not only that what I started I had to complete and do well - there is nothing wrong with that - but that I had to do it extremely well, no matter at what cost, and do it now or yesterday rather than today. Mother was an idealist. She could do no wrong. All her ideals were correct. Subconsciously, I had to imitate her, though I never admitted it to myself. In the end she always did and achieved what she had set out to do. Only now do I realise that she was extremely stubborn without ever appearing to be so. I also adopted this trait of character. Often both these traits of character served me well. Without this determination and stubbornness, I would perhaps not be walking and thinking clearly. But now it is time to become a little more easy-going, not too stubborn and inflexible; to trust more in the power of the All-Pervasive Energy and to accept that if I am open enough, it will point out the right path, instead of my going along a straight line which may sometimes do harm when one least expects it.

A few months after father's death, on a bright summer afternoon, my ex-wife rang.

"Did you read the paper?"

"No, what happened?"

"Wojtek is dead. Wojtek was murdered."

"Are you sure? Papers often exaggerate. What paper?"

I just could not believe it.

"The article does not give many details, but it looks to me that there is no doubt."

Wojtek was my best friend. To me there was something very special about him. Now I think I know what it was.

We had been together in college and graduated at the same time in the same subject. We both became lecturers in physical chemistry though in different aspects. His doctorate had been in chemistry and mine in metallurgy. He proposed many modifications in content and methodology of teaching; they were rejected, so he applied for a professorship in the United Nations. He raised the standard of several chemistry departments in Third World countries all over the world. He did much valuable work, yet to me he had always been courting death. When in Algeria he stayed there during the revolution and left only at the last moment, after all other UNESCO personnel had been evacuated.

When in the University of Amman, Jordan, he at first refused to leave during the Palestinian revolution in the early seventies. Bullets flew through his flat and I saw the holes when I visited him in 1973. But Wojtek stayed. One day he was asked to hand over the keys to his car to the revolutionary force. He refused and was arrested. After days, when he was questioned by someone in a high position, he said he was Polish - true in the sense that his parents were Polish, though he had come to England as a child and was British.

"Polish? So you are a Communist? Your country is part of the Big Brotherhood."

The Palestinians had at the time strong communist connections.

"Well," Wojtek answered. "I was born in Poland, but not all Poles..."

They had not let him finish.

"Go home. We are all fighting for liberty; we are all fighting for the same cause."

No further discussion. They had other business to attend to. Wojtek returned to his wife and two daughters in Amman. They had nearly given up hope of ever seeing him again.

Now he did leave Amman, but he returned before any other of the UNESCO personnel. There was still much unrest, but the University had opened.

"My students need me," was all he was prepared to say, when I visited him later. He had invited me to give some lectures on a topic on which I had recently published some work. He was obviously liked by his students and other professors.

Soon thereafter his wife died. I helped him to make arrangements for his daughters to go to a boarding school in England.

Later he met a most charming Filipino girl, Evelyn, whom he married in 1977. He had another daughter with her. When the baby was six months old, his two other daughters, now thirteen and seventeen, were visiting him during their summer vacation. He was in Uganda and it was the time of Idi Amin Dada, civil war, chaos and murder. He should have left earlier. His belongings were packed, but he left it too late.

One night he heard noises on the ground floor, went down and saw men in uniform sawing through the metal gratings of a window. He switched on the light. They shot at him. His wife with the baby in her arms came down. They came in, shot him again, cut her mouth with a bayonet, took the keys to the car and left.

Wojtek died.

I rang Uganda. I do not remember to whom I got through. I think I also spoke to Evelyn. I was prepared to fly down and help with the children, thinking she might have lost her nerves completely. There was someone from the BBC there who was making all the arrangements for the family to be repatriated to England. I was told on what flight they would arrive.

I had met Evelyn only briefly once before. I was on my course in Switzerland when they were married in England. From the airport they went to Wojtek's mother's and stepfather's house. Wojtek and his brother Mark, who now worked in Japan, had built in the roof space a little flat for their use when on holiday. This was where Evelyn was going to stay until she was ready to decide how to continue her life.

A few days later the coffin with Wojtek's remains arrived. His brother asked me to hold the funeral oration. "Keep your voice steady," he told me. "Pretend you are making an announcement at a railway station. It will be easier that way for his wife." He was right of course. But it was difficult to outline his life just briefly and not become involved in any personal reminiscences. Somehow I did it. My last words were, "He was my best friend, the best friend many of us had."

There was more truth to it than I realised at that time. He was a highly evolved being.

A few more days passed and then the telephone rang. It was Evelyn's voice, very unhappy and half crying.

"Tadek, come and get me. I am packed. Please come."

It was not the time to ask what had happened. The desperation in her voice was obvious.

"I shall be there in minutes. If there is no traffic, fifteen at the most."

I got into the car. When I arrived, she was waiting outside with her baby. I brought them to my home.

Slowly things came out, though I shall never know all the details. She was a Filipino. Her character, to me a very beautiful one, was very different from the average central European character. Her parents-in-law could not understand her and did not like her. She could not take it any more. Her husband, Wojtek, had once told her that his friend Tadeusz, myself, was often a conceited bastard, but if she was ever in need of something, or if something happened to himself, she should turn to him. She did.

She stayed with us for six months until she decided how to continue her life. She went first to Manila and her family, and then onto various other UN assignments, all over the world. Our house has remained her only "permanent" home. Every year and between assignments she stays there. Recently she bought a small house in London, but she does not like it. She still stays in our house. Kathryn, her daughter, now sixteen and a beautiful woman, always had a key to our home. Even when we are not in London, she and her mother sometimes stay there.

Once when we talked about Wojtek with Evelyn she complained, "Why did he leave me? Why does he never show himself, in my dreams or as a spirit, and give me advice?" At another time she said that he had told her, "When I die I shall not return to this earth again."

By the time she told me this I was beginning to understand many things which earlier would have seemed absurd. The spirit which inhabited Wojtek's body was a highly elevated one. It was his last incarnation on this earth. He needed to experience only a few more things, perhaps a violent death was amongst them, before he would graduate to a different level, one we know nothing about. Sometimes, but rarely, we consciously know things our spirit knows. It was during one of those moments that

Wojtek said that "he" would never return to this earth again.

In 1980 I was offered a professorship in California. In a narrow field of corrosion I was a recognised specialist, which they seemed to appreciate in spite of the fact that in London I was considered incapable of lecturing after my accident; my previous lecturing abilities seemed attractive to them. For once I hesitated; I was not a person in full health and America can be tricky if something goes wrong with one's health. Why the hesitation? I had never been worried about my health before. Several months later, to the great surprise of my friends, I rejected the offer. In the meantime, with the help of the bank, who still trusted me as a result of my pre-accident dealings, and an acquaintance who had been a manager of a pub, I purchased a public house near Oxford. It was a great bargain. My nose for a good deal had not yet gone. I suppose it is still there now, but I just do not wish to use it.

I spent a few weeks living in the pub to make sure it started on the right footing. I was prepared to eat there - I always liked eating in pubs - but I never went behind the bar. Why? Snobbishness?

After my first night there Elizabeth, who had returned from Cambridge to São Paulo in Brazil by then, came to my mind. Every single day I thought of her. I knew she was the woman I should marry. Completely crazy, I knew nothing about the girl. I had seen her for two days nearly two years ago. I had never thought of her since then. I could not understand it.

I fished out her address which, being a polite lady, she had given me after her stay in my house, with the statement that if I ever came to São Paulo she would gladly show me around. My letter to her was as close to a proposal of marriage as a letter can be, without the words "Will you marry me?"; she kept the letter but did not answer it. The "absurd" knowledge that I had to marry the girl passed as though it had never existed. For seven more years she did not come into my mind.

Have not most of us come across or experienced this? A thought comes to us for no reason that we can think of, does not want to let go and then suddenly vanishes, only to come again for no obvious reason. Psychologists, even neurologists, have tried to explain this, none successfully, and none agree with each other. If we accept that we often know minutes or seconds in advance that someone is going to telephone us, or a mother suddenly feels something dramatic has happened to her child who is a thousand miles away, then we have to accept that a form of thought transfer exists. This is not a currently measurable energy. It should not then be too difficult to accept that immeasurable energies exist, which emanate from sources other than human bodies.

I began to realise that my relationship with Morena, though satisfying on some levels, was making me neurotic and literally driving me to drink. I felt I could only have a permanent relationship with a woman if I married her. She enjoyed my company and enjoyed going to bed with me. Often we had a wild and satisfying time. She enjoyed travelling with me. We slept in our tent high in the Alps with cowbells waking us when the sun rose. We drove through fog and snow, and stopped in romantic inns when the weather prevented us from going further. We stopped beside bubbling brooks in the Pyrenees. Once when the gearbox of our car exploded near one of the few remaining deserted Mediterranean beaches, we rented a beautiful flat right on the beach. We spent days lying on the deserted sand or on the flat roof naked, making love, eating vast quantities of salad with garlic, so that we and all our clothes stank of garlic, even after a new gearbox was flown in and we had returned to London.

Fortunately I had insured myself well, as I always do, so that the repairs, hotel and other incidental expenses were born by the insurance company. Recently, whenever I needed something it came from somewhere. People thought I was still wealthy. I was not. Things just came to me when I needed them. I have now learned that when you are in tune with the universe it contrives to help whenever necessary.

We went to California to visit my godmother and drove through the desert to the Grand Canyon, to me one of the most glorious and impressive places in the world. In Las Vegas we entered our hotel, the Aladdin, from the garage at the back. This meant going through a long corridor with flashing lights, lined on both sides with one-armed bandits. At each sat another machine with a semi-human distorted face, pulling down a lever every seven seconds. Occasionally the jingle of silver pieces and a grimace of pleasure on a distorted face was illuminated by flashing red lights.

"This is what hell must be like," I said loudly and felt a shiver of horror running down my back.

At the reception desk we were handed a key. The Circus Hotel had made the booking for us since they were full due to their special offer of $30 per room. They had an arrangement with other hotels that anybody they could not put up would pay no more when transferred to them.

The reception area was luxurious. But when we got out of the lift on the fourth floor our breath was taken away. The most beautiful luxurious carpet lined the floor of the wide corridor. The doors to the rooms were of carved hardwood. A feeling of not only opulence, but of a tastefully designed modern, but yet not too modern, palace. The door to our room opened smoothly onto an anteroom. On the left was a bathroom full of mirrors and marble, which did not jar but was simply breathtaking. The bedroom itself could be taken for the set of a James Bond film, a place designed to forget the real world and give oneself to the corporal pleasures of this life. No sounds from the outside world were heard, just a gentle whisper from the air conditioning. The temperature was adjusted so that one could lie comfortably, naked, on the six foot bed and cover oneself with an exquisitely delicate soft sheet. Just as the corridor lined with gambling machines through which we had passed when entering, with its flashing lights, noises, sporadic exclamations, jingling of silver and intense, to me diabolic, faces reminded me of hell, so the room in which we were could be an antechamber to heaven.

In the morning, after we rang for breakfast, a trolley arrived with a huge flame on which fresh pancakes were prepared, whilst we lay as God had created us, covered by a light sheet and enveloped by soft music. Again everything was arranged to arouse our fantasies.

It was good that at that time I was not yet affected by the electromagnetic waves which must have been smothering us, emanating from all the machines which kept the room in such "perfect" climatic condition. Years later when I came for the third visit to Las Vegas, this time to the newly built Excalibur, perhaps not quite so elegant but equally comfortable, I felt as though somebody was gently hammering at me all the time, and was looking forward to getting out again. So much had happened during the intervening ten years; my sensitivity had become so very different.

From Las Vegas we drove again through the desert and visited what looked from a distance like a golden sun. An enormous globe was illuminated from several sides by concave mirrors reflecting the light from the real sun, an experiment using sunlight to generate power. This was something I had been interested in since my school days, when atomic power stations were about to be introduced. I felt at the time that this was an irresponsible act. What were they going to do with the waste products? What if one of them went out of control? If all the money spent on this development was used to harness the natural power of the sun, the wind, the waves, and the water, and if heat pumps were developed we could have all the power we needed safely. If a teenager could see this, why could scientists, economists and politicians not see it? Was vested interest governing the world? Now I know that it was, but then I found it difficult to believe. I was an idealist. I do not think I changed. I always wanted everybody to be healthy and happy, though my definition and understanding of health and happiness may have changed.

Further on our way towards the Sequoia Forest we saw a "town" of windmills, again used to produce power. I was pleased that serious work on non-polluting power generation was done. I had read about it. It gave me pleasure to see it working in practice.

In the Sequoia Forest we slept in a hut among the trees and went for long walks, for me a glorious experience. I felt good and relaxed, though at the time I had no idea why. Others too felt the same, but few put much thought into why this was so. Were the trees emanating something or was it just because we were away from the noise, machinery and cables carrying electricity? Much was beginning to be written about all this, but even those who read it, some with interest, did not put much thought into it.

Many years later, when I returned with my sons, I could again sense this relaxing effect. I went there once more with my second wife. This time she once felt an "energy" so strongly near a tree which had fallen over that she asked me to take a photograph. I had learned by then to trust her feelings. When we developed the film there was a mist effect in the area where she felt something. In another few years I learnt to see an energy mantle, surrounding in particular old trees, but also some younger ones provided they were in fairly natural surroundings. In towns I still cannot see this "energy mantle" around trees; presumably it is less intense.

After Morena and I returned to Long Beach to my godmother, who loved me as much as my mother did, I felt the tremendous difference between the "wilderness" or natural surrounding and town so intensely that I could not stop a continuous feeling of tenseness. With hindsight I realise that it was this that triggered off the first serious difficulties between us.

Morena flew directly back to London; I went via Miami in Florida where I visited some friends. Again there was the feeling of tenseness in crowded areas, but of relaxation when they drove me out to the Everglades.

CHAPTER 4

The Dawning
If you really want something to occur, and it is right for you, then it will.

"Will you marry me?" I asked Morena again.

"No," was the answer as it had been several times before.

Why?

"I don't know, perhaps later."

All other matters we could discuss, but not this.

With hindsight I realise the reason. My feelings for her, which I called love, were more than an infatuation; they were an addiction, but they were not love. She was more perceptive than I. She knew instinctively, even if she could not verbalise it, that we were not meant for each other.

At the time I felt that I was about to become impotent or simply go crazy. I even frequently stayed away from my own house, became confused and went for lonely walks at night. I knew this could not continue. Yet when we did make love, which became less and less frequent, I still enjoyed it immensely. There is a great difference between addiction, even when combined with liking and respect, and love.

In the latter, if reciprocated, the partner can do no wrong. It is difficult if not impossible to get angry with him or her. An intuitive understanding exists. One knows that one has and has been chosen, and therefore has a responsibility to keep the other person happy in spite of all outside interference. One never thinks what is wrong with him or her. He or she is as he or she is, and one abides by it. It is what one has chosen.

The theory that true love means that one side completes the other, that each is a "C" and together they form an "O", is a dangerous one. It may work for a time, but one side or the other, or both, will try to dominate. They will forget that they reached a fullness only as a result of joining the other. Sometimes one side is prepared to annihilate its ego and then a kind of happy relationship can exist. More frequently the dominated side resents being considered inferior and a situation of constant tension develops. One side or the other begins to seek satisfaction elsewhere. Even the dominating side may get bored with dominating, will lose respect for the partner and seek someone else who may be more assertive, or interesting, or simply satisfying.

In arranged marriages neither side had illusions of a "full" relationship and, therefore, did not mind if it was not all that fairy tales said it could be.

In mutually desired marriages of the type where one felt an irresistible attraction for the other, which usually meant that each needed something from the other, two "C's" forming an "O", it was usually but by no means always the husband who dominated. Often he became bored and started looking for satisfaction elsewhere.

Today in many western countries, the woman has become emancipated. Either she dominates the family, and wishes it to be known that she does, or will rebel if the husband wants to dominate. In both cases they forget that they chose each other to "complete" each other. A separation is the result in two thirds of modern marriages.

True love flourishes and lasts best if each partner is a complete entity, does not need the other to survive and realises that the other is equally complete, perhaps complete in a different way but beautiful as an individual just as each of two complementary colours can shine together as a bright and beautiful white, so one circle superimposed on the other will shine as a brilliant white single circle. It is often more powerful and more illuminating than either of its components. That is why some couples will draw other people to themselves, and make them feel comfortable and content. They illuminate everything in a bright neutral light, which does not distract, and which can be trusted and relied on to show the truth.

Morena probably realised, even if only subconsciously, that together we would not create this white light. Perhaps neither of us was yet fully mature; perhaps she knew that even when we matured we would not be "complementary colours".

Since none of this had yet penetrated my consciousness, I went in desperation to a psychiatrist for advice. Perhaps I needed psychiatric help, perhaps not. Today I do not believe in the majority of them; I believe that if you are uncertain, sit back and withdraw for a day or a week, and frequently the answer will come to you. A discussion with friends may help, but a psychiatrist too often causes a dependence on outside help, a relinquishing of one's own responsibility. There are few psychiatrists who have the right attitude. These will give advice, perhaps a brief course of treatment, but make it quite clear that the patient will in future be able to come to his own conclusions and must not continually return for more advice.

Psychology and psychiatry, orthodox or Jungian, should expand our mind, not settle it. The aim of the consulting room should often be a revolution, not a place in which we learn to cope with life. Psychology is usually of the world. The puzzle in therapy should not mainly be "How did I get this way?" but "What does my 'angel' want to tell me?"

My psychiatrist saw me twice and her advice was quite clear. With my perception of the situation and my present mental physical state, if I did not immediately separate myself from Morena I might literally, within days, suffer a heart attack. I suggested I would leave my house and admitted that I had had such thoughts before. That in her opinion would be the worst thing I could do. I would leave my last bit of "firm earth". I had lost wife, children, career, memory and money. Under no circumstances must I voluntarily lose more. I must build up. My only chance if I wished to survive was to ask Morena to leave me immediately. In her opinion it was a matter of life and death.

So Morena and I separated.

I shall be for ever grateful to her. During the first few months after my now ex-wife left me, Morena gave me an incredible feeling of well-being. I remember feeling frequently, "If I now die, I shall not mind. I have experienced absolute bliss."

She did not want to marry me, and this gave me the opportunity to meet the person who was the exactly correct shade of complementary colour and with whom I could jointly achieve the brilliant white light which changed my life in every respect.

In 1985 Aleksander was twenty-three and Marius nineteen years old. I took both my sons to California as I felt it would be good for them to widen their horizons and good for all three of us to get to know each other better. Though we saw each other frequently in London it was always only for a few hours. We hired a car at the airport in Los Angeles; although all of us had driving licences, Marius was not allowed to drive since the car hire company had a policy not to hire out to anyone under twenty-one.

We made my godmother's house in Longbeach our headquarters. Again we drove across the desert, starting at 5.00 in the morning, towards the Grand Canyon. On the way we saw London Bridge which had been dismantled in London and rebuilt in the middle of the desert. Part of the Colorado River had been diverted to flow under it. An English pub, a red London telephone box and some London-type houses were supposed to recreate a London atmosphere in the middle of nowhere. A tourist attraction? Not overly successful. A desire to find and recreate roots? Possibly. Mock castles and mock historical battles have become quite popular in the USA. Is this a sign that the American culture leaves the local population unsatisfied, that money, which is what the majority of local inhabitants seem to treasure most, does not bring them the deep satisfaction which a poor painter, musician, teacher or just "helper" might feel? During the last few years more and more people feel that to give is often more satisfying than to receive or take.

Something is changing dramatically. Is it too late or too slow to avoid a catastrophe?

Sitting in the car together, just the three of us, gave us a chance to open up to each other. Both my sons were very bright as children. Aleksander could read and speak three languages when he was three years old. In his initial school years he was always first in his class, yet in his last years he seemed to stop working. He was still good but only as a result of his intelligence. His work input was low. Although he did well in his A-levels and could have gone to most universities, he decided to take a sabbatical year and work in industry, followed by a second sabbatical. He did extremely well in his electronics firm.

During our chats in the car he said that he probably did not want to go to university because he felt that he could not compete with his father, with all his fellowships and always doing better than others. This may not have been the only reason, but it showed to me clearly that a parent should never overwhelm his children by stressing his achievements and implying, if not saying directly, that only by academic, financial, artistic or any other achievement, can one become a really valuable person.

As I now understand the world, the opposite may be true. A person who tries to develop his intellect to too great an extent, in whatever field, may become narrow-minded and unable to appreciate the deeper and more important values of life; may find it difficult to understand the reasons and final purpose of life, and may therefore become cold to his surroundings and not find the deep satisfaction which can only be obtained when one realises that there is more to life than a beautiful house, a fat bank account, a beautiful partner and being asked out to social events.

The sun was shining relentlessly as we continued our journey through the desert. The air inside the car became unbearably hot. Then we realised the air conditioning had stopped working. We stopped and got the gallon container of water out of the boot; we had been well advised never to travel through the desert without plenty of water. Aleksander took the wheel and Marius sat next to him; I poured some water over them from time to time. We continued our chat. It helped me to take one of the many large steps which changed my life.

"Father, father," said Marius, "look back."

There was a police car right on our tail, with lights flashing. Aleksander also glanced at the mirror.

"Oh!" he said. "We are being followed."

"Perhaps we should stop," was my remark.

The police car stopped behind us.

"What evil deed are we guilty of?" I asked. From my accent it was obvious I was not an American.

He ignored me with a polite smile and turned to Aleksander, the driver.

"Why did you not look into the mirror? You would have seen us following you for some time."

"The mirror is in an awkward position. I couldn't see you. What have we done?"

"You were going 65 miles per hour. The limit is 55."

We all knew this very well, but on an empty desert road did not take it seriously.

"Sorry, officer," he said. "In England 70 miles is the limit. I suppose I drove the way I normally drive."

"Oh, you come from England. I heard they drive faster than we do."

He took out his book and calculated the fine, but then smiled and said,

"Remember in future where you are. I shall let you go this time."

When it was my turn to drive I looked carefully into the mirror, but drove again at 60 to 65 miles per hour. We had not seen a car for many minutes when Marius noticed a police car in the distance on the other side of the motorway. To be on the safe side I slowed down.

A minute or two later, "Dad, why is the police car chasing us?"

Just then I also noticed a police car with flashing lights coming round the bend. I stopped, got out of the car and smiled.

"What have I done? I was driving no more than 55 miles per hour."

"Yes, now, but when you passed our radar point you were recorded doing 67."

"Oh! I must not have looked at the speedometer. In England 70 is the limit."

"I know but here it is 55."

Out came the book again and he asked for my driving licence. "This time we shall pay," I thought.

"Can I pay by cheque? We do not have very much cash on us."

"Oh, no, you don't have to pay for a month. Pay when you get back to Los Angeles." He blinked with his left eye. "I have to give you a ticket; you were recorded on radar."

"But we are not going to be here in a month. Can't I pay by cheque?"

His left eye twitched again significantly. "I know. Pay later." A grin spread over his face.

The light dawned. He did not want me to pay. Not all American policemen are what most films show them to be or perhaps it was our friendly attitude which made them react the way they did. It confirms my belief that one must never generalise. If Hitler and a million Germans, or Stalin, were bad that does not mean that all Germans or Russians are bad. Frequently it is also the attitude which one adopts towards a person, even if it is only an attitude of mind, not shown by facial expression or intonation, that makes a person react one way or another.

Experiments have shown that even plants grow better when their owner thinks with love about them. We all know that some people have "green fingers". Anything they plant, or grow in their house or garden, grows better than things planted by others who water and feed their plants in exactly the same way.

Why should human beings be less perceptive than plants are?

The heat in the car remained unbearable. There was no easy way of repairing the air conditioning, but we were happy and therefore did not notice the heat as much as we would have done if our mood was different.

From that time our relationship, never bad, became even closer. Though I still missed not having seen them every day and participating in their maturing for the last eight years, I no longer resented it.

What I had learned above all during the trip with my sons is that when trying to bring up children one should never drain their energy and their initiative consciously or subconsciously while correcting them. The children should always be included in conversations and never spoken of as if they were not present. Whatever outside commitments a parent might have, he must find time to pay full attention to his children. If a grandparent or other relation has to take care of children, then it must be done with the full understanding and permission of the children.

Children should learn from adults, not from other children, otherwise they will start forming gangs, learn from each other and, depending on their character, may become wild creatures, taking their revenge on a society which did not give them the affection and care which they required.

Children as well as adults have both a female and male side. In the case of a boy he has to learn to integrate his female side. In the first instance he will attempt to do this by being attracted to his mother. He will want her near him all the time. The girl will want her father to be close to her. This is because the other sex's energy will complement the child's own energy. A boy may think that his mother is magic and able to supply his every desire. This may set up a conflict. It will cause him to try and manipulate her into giving him what he desires. Ideally the parents should explain that they are not magicians, just ordinary human beings trying to do their best. Then the child will absorb the parents' energy, particularly the energy of the opposite-sex parent as of an ordinary human being resulting from all his positive and negative aspects. This will make it easier for the child, when growing up and beginning to search for a partner of the opposite sex, to look not only for those characteristics which result from that partner's sex and which therefore complement his own sexual characteristics, but to look for general characteristics which he finds attractive. It is important for the child to understand what the character of his opposite-sex friends really is. This will enable him (or her) to outgrow any fantasy he may have about that sex.

A parent who is a friend of the child, in that child's opinion, will make it much easier for a child to break these sex fantasies, or not have there at all. The child becomes more complete. It can still have a beautiful romance, but it will be a romance based on a fullness which he possesses, and not on a desire to attain this fullness. It will therefore be much more satisfying and lasting.

With the experience which I have gained since the conversation with my sons more than ten years ago, I realise that we are all rapidly growing out of the co-dependence most of us much relied on.

When I look at young people now, particularly those who have been given a sensible background by their parents, I feel that we are becoming much more self-reliant.

Unfortunately those children who run in gangs, to replace what their parents did not give them, also become more self-reliant and the self-reliance shows itself by aggressiveness towards not only those who do not belong to the gang but also to others within the gang.

The desire for individual completeness, rather than co-dependence, shows itself in economic and political fields as well. Small units or provinces no longer want to be part of a bigger unit, if their joining this unit was forced upon them by outside circumstances or brutal force. They want to experience their own completeness. They will join together again into units larger than ever before, but this joining will be the result of their own free will, firstly because they will realise that co-operation with and not dependence upon their neighbour gives them more energy to enjoy life and to do what they know they would like to do, and secondly because they will know that co-operation rather than competition with the neighbouring country leads not only to greater prosperity but also to a greater fullness and beauty. Finally, co-operation on a world-wide scale will become a universal desire. We will realise that we all have the same desires, whether black or white, Jewish or Arabic, European or Chinese. We shall realise that if one fights for something which is obtainable only at the expense of the other, both shall in the long run be losers.

History has shown this clearly, but history has never been a great teacher. It is evolution that causes changes. I believe that we are now undergoing a very rapid spiritual evolution. Much destruction will still occur, rather like the skin of a teenager which bursts and becomes covered with pimples through which the toxins escape before his skin becomes smooth and beautiful. The extent of destruction will depend on how quickly we learn what life's priorities are. We should also realise that our thoughts, and not only our actions, can cause physical occurrences.

I tried to see my ex-wife more frequently after this trip by inviting her to my house together with our children, but she refused. We did occasionally meet in her house and once or twice in a restaurant. At the time I did not understand. Now perhaps I do. I was the wrong person for her. By marrying her, I had caused her life to become, from her point of view, empty. She had complained several times whilst we were still married that, "There must be more to life." I did not understand. I thought I gave her everything: love, at least what I then understood by love, a pleasant social life, freedom to travel alone if she so wished, a chance to study and, when I started in business, a directorship in each of our companies.

Yet I obviously did not give her what she needed. I never knew what it was. Now I think I do. Neither of us was a complete "O", a complete circle, and I was not even the "C", the half circle, which she required to make an "O". It is only when two "Os" come together that the symbol for infinity, , is obtained and an infinitely full relationship may result.

Fortunately for me I was prepared to learn. Though financially I lost everything, I gained in experience and fullness with every new relationship I experienced. Perhaps this was so because I was prepared to be open; perhaps I was learning to harbour no ill will to anybody and to love unconditionally. The last, which took me many years, is I believe the most important aspect of this life. Only unconditional love can make a relationship really beautiful.

Morena lived first with her sister and then bought a flat. We saw each other frequently, and even made love both in her flat and my house. I asked her once again to marry me, with the by now customary answer. I told her then that this was the last time I was doing so. If ever she changed her mind she would have to ask me. Our lovemaking became better and then faded out slowly.

I began to think seriously of opening a centre for unorthodox healing, the type that put me on my feet. I would have to find someone who had the necessary financial background and someone who had the necessary experience. Spirituality began to become a factor in my life. I went to priests to discuss it, but they were of no help except for one, a Jesuit. He listened to me as I explained my attitude to life and the fact that I was living with a girl to whom I was not married and never could marry in the Catholic Church since it permitted no divorce. My admission that I went to church only when I felt like it, and had not been to confession for some twenty years, did not seem to worry him.

"There are many ways to God. Imagine Him as the top of a pyramid. You can get to the top in any way you feel is right for you. Some do it by going to church and confession. It is a good way. There are others. If you do and feel what you say you do, continue with it. You will get to the top as quickly or perhaps quicker than some who go to church every Sunday."

I spoke of the possibility of annulling my marriage, so that I could marry again in the church. "If you want to it can probably be done, but with your attitude to life does it really matter?"

"If I marry again," I answered, "my future wife may well wish to marry in church."

"Do you really think so? Once you find the right person?"

This was all a little above me at that time. I did not realise that amongst Roman Catholics such attitudes existed. Above all I did not know what he really meant. Now I do. I know that the really good marriages are made in "heaven" whatever that is, and not on earth. Here they are only confirmed.

I went through the introductory procedure of an annulment of my church marriage. The priest conducting it was very sympathetic. Everything was recorded on tape. He explained to me that whether I or my wife was the cause of the breakdown of our marriage was technically irrelevant. All that took two two-hour sessions.

Then came the crunch. "Are you prepared to say that your wife married you because this would elevate her position socially or financially? Did she marry you because of your money or standing in society? Do not answer now; think about it. Did she marry you knowing that she did not want children, and it was you who persuaded her to have children?"

I opened my mouth to answer.

"No," he said. "Do not answer; think about it."

There was something else. I have forgotten what. I knew he was giving me a chance to say one of the things which would make an annulment possible. I was not prepared to lie, or even bend the truth. When we married, I thought my wife loved me according to what little understanding of love we then had. I still think so..She may not have been keen on having children at that time, but I had no doubt that she would want them later. I was shocked by this attitude of "the Church", though I am sure the priest meant well.

"No," I answered. "When she married me she loved me, not my future career nor my money; I had none. She had no objection to children; we did not discuss it. If these are the only reasons and not the fact that she does not love me now, and lives with somebody else, then I prefer to rest my case."

Later I was informed that I had not shown the right reasons for the annulment of my marriage.

Being a business consultant did not appeal to me. I was prepared to give advice to friends, but not to charge for my work. Why? I know I had a flair for it. I could not be officially employed because my memory was sometimes unreliable and I became confused, but I suppose I could have acted as an independent consultant and prayed that I did not get confused during an important part of work. I usually had good warning before any confusion set in. No, it was something else. Whenever I helped others I did very well; when I tried to do something for myself I did not do well. It was as though an outside force was telling me, "There is something else you have to do."

I took an interest in natural heath clinics; after all, one such clinic had put me on my feet, so perhaps I should help others in some similar way. I discussed setting up a health centre with others. At that time I felt a health centre, offering massage, water treatments, yoga, homeopathy, herbs and diets, had something missing. What this something was I did not quite know.

I went to a "Festival of Mind, Body and Spirit" and found it fascinating. There was Kirlian photography. A photograph was taken of your hand when placed on a photographic plate underneath which there was passing a high-potential high-frequency electrical current. The hand appeared on the photographic plate with "streamers" coming out of it. Most "streamers" are so close that an aura seems to surround the hand. An analysis of those streamers shows much about your psychological make up at the time, about your attitudes and perhaps why you have them.

I had had a Kirlian photograph taken before, in Switzerland by an orthodox doctor. I did it at the time because I wanted to know more about this phenomenon. He did tell me at the time that I had stomach problems, which I did, and that they were not the result of my anatomic make up but of nervous tension. I knew this was probably true. He seemed to combine physiological diagnosis with a psychological one. In London they stressed only the psychological aspects. I learned later the two aspects required the use of different techniques. The psychological analysis required the placing of the whole palm, and with some practitioners also the foot, on the photographic plate. The physiological diagnosis was facilitated if only the tips of the ten fingers were placed on the plate.

During a demonstration I observed how a person, chosen at random, was regressed by hypnotic suggestions to the moment she was born and beyond it to a time when she was in her mother's womb. She knew that she would become a female child and that her father wanted a male child, and feared that he might not love her. Her voice had changed from the adult one she normally used to a child's and then a baby's voice as she was being regressed. I was sure that she was not pretending. I spoke with her afterwards; she too was surprised how her voice had changed. She really felt all she said. I only half believed her. I had no reason not to, but I was simply not ready for it. I have since then often witnessed others not believing what they were seeing, or being certain that they were being misled and that it was magic or hypnotism which caused them to see things which were not facts.

During another workshop we were gently led to a point where most of us experienced what the lecturer said was a past life experience.

I saw myself on my deathbed in a monastery in, I was sure (how I do not know) ancient Egypt. My present elder son Aleksander was the abbot who came to visit me; also present was another monk who was my present younger son Marius. Nobody was telling me what to see and nobody was looking at me suggesting anything. I could accept the experience as something I really remembered or reject it as a silly phantasy. I was not sure

49

what to do. I stored it for future reference.

I attended a lecture by Mathew Manning, a well-known healer at that time. I do not remember the details, but I do remember some examples he gave of the effect of thought on actual occurrences. He gave references of some of the work done which I could check. It impressed me because I began to realise that some of the "miracles" I had witnessed at Friedborn Sanatorium, including my own rapid healing, when orthodox medicine left me as a cripple, were not inexplicable.

My interest in natural health clinics increased. I even designed an outline of one which would include a healer such as Mathew Manning. I sent the proposal to him, but had no answer.

During the next exhibition, which I think was the Healing Arts, I noticed a stand of the National Federation of Spiritual Healers. Lilla Bek was signing a book which she had recently published called *What colour are you?* I chatted briefly with her and found that she was born to Polish parents, as I was. Philippa Puller, a co-author of some of Lilla's books, asked me whether I wanted some "healing".

I was beginning to accept that healing by nonphysical means was possible and that perhaps it had contributed to my return to health. Yet to sit down on a chair in full public view and have someone move her hands over me, without quite touching me, made me feel very self-conscious. I experienced nothing, yet I agreed to see Philippa in her own house. I found her an attractive lady, certainly not what I expected a "spiritual healer" to be. There was nothing "spiritual", in the sense I understood it, about her.

Again I found no "healing" effect. I frequently had a pain in my hip which was beginning to be arthritic again. After two sessions, Philippa very rightly suggested that my scientific training made it difficult for me to accept anything that could not be "scientifically" proven. She suggested some biofeedback experiments. Elsewhere I had some electrodes put on my head and found that by concentrating or relaxing or switching off I could change my brainwaves. The presence of a healer facilitated this change. Here was something that resonated with what I had been taught.

I attended a healing course run by Philippa. We practised healing on each other and on outsiders (friends), as well as distant healing.

After some time Philippa phoned me. "Can you come before the others? I want to discuss something with you."

"Certainly. I'll come an hour earlier."

When I arrived we had tea and Philippa asked, "When you do your healing do you touch your patient?"

"Not usually, but sometimes I suppose I do. Why?"

"I told you some people feel invaded when touched; it is best just to stroke the aura."

"All right, but why are you stressing this now?"

"Miss X rang me after our session and complained that she felt literally sick after your healing. She felt that you were stripping off her clothes and invading her. You have to be extremely careful; people are very sensitive when they undergo healing."

A few weeks later, Philippa rang me again.

"Miss Y complained that she felt you were sexually assaulting her. What are you doing?"

I did not go to the next few healing sessions. I was supposed to do good, not harm. Then it dawned on me.

Sometimes I felt that whatever the woman patient's complaint was, it was caused by frustration, and lack of sex and male company. If she could but find these, her various symptoms would vanish. Both ladies must have picked up these background thoughts of mine.

It taught me three things. Firstly, that if ladies could feel sick after exposing themselves to my thoughts, they could equally feel better if I had had different thoughts. Healing was therefore certainly a fact.

Secondly, I had to be very careful what I thought when I did some healing.

Thirdly, I could certainly do things to people without touching them. I could harm and therefore also heal them.

Later I learned to blank myself out and try to act just as a channel for healing energy, which I believe exists everywhere, and focus it onto the patient.

I know I have removed many small ailments such as headaches, backaches and rheumatic aches. Once the mother of a friend, who required massage twice a week to remove her backache, asked me to try some healing on her. It worked. She had no pain for several weeks. I never tried to heal anything dramatic, in others. I liked helping others in all possible ways, talking to them, arranging things for them and lending them money when I could afford it, but I felt a reluctance to perform "spiritual healing". Somehow I felt this was not my calling, at least not the way it was done by the National Federation of Spiritual Healers.

I thought I could help people without telling them that I was doing so, by concentrating and looking at them. I could certainly heal some of my own problems.

I was suffering then from arthritis of my left hip which had been shattered during my accident. I had been told some years before that I ought to have a hip replacement. My answer was to go to Friedborn in Bad Sackingen and the pain diminished. Now I had myself X-rayed again and was told that operations were now even safer than before, that my arthritis was advanced and that I should decide on a hip replacement. I did not. I bought myself a tape by Mathew Manning which took one through a visualisation procedure which he claimed would reduce or remove the arthritis.

After relaxing my whole body starting with the feet, going through the body to my scalp and then down again, and saying, "My feet are relaxed, my calves are relaxed," etc., I visualised the white blood corpuscles cleaning my hip joint and then removing the inflammation, and then the red blood corpuscles bringing more oxygen to it and thus making the missing cartilage grow. After twenty minutes twice a day and some four weeks the pain had gone.

Over ten years have passed since I first did this self-healing. Sometimes I forget for a few weeks and the pain comes back. In a month, sometimes just a week, I have it under control. At first I had myself X-rayed again after the pain stopped. The arthritis seemed to have receded. Now I do not bother, though during my last BUPA general examination, the doctor who examined me happened to be a retired orthopaedist and I was strongly advised to have an operation. Major problems could have already arisen. I was lucky they had not; he said that I could not expect to continue to be lucky for many more years to come. I am now sixty-two, and I expect to be lucky for many more years.

CHAPTER 5

A Year to Remember: the Introduction to Bliss
Those who have the courage to search and look will find that the Energy will lead them, if they allow it to do so.

In 1985 my oldest girlfriend, whom I called Mucke, telephoned. It was the evening of 5th September. She lived in Heidelberg, six hundred miles and a channel away from London where I lived.

"Come to my birthday. I am preparing a big party. I have some Brazilians staying with me and they have promised to prepare a Brazilian feast. We will have it out on the lawn. There will be thirty or more friends."

Her birthday was on 9th September, in four days. I would have to leave the day after next, which gave plenty of time to get a Green Card and ferry ticket. I preferred to drive rather than fly; it made me more independent.

I had met Mucke when she was five and I was four years old in 1937. Mother, our maid and I were going to Zopot, a seaside town. I, as always, wandered up and down the carriage. Inside one compartment was what seemed to me a very desirable specimen of the opposite sex. I opened the door and asked a lady whom I presumed to be her mother - she was her aunt - whether I might kiss the young lady's hand. Having been given permission I introduced myself and fulfilled my desire. Then I asked whether I might bring my mother and introduce her. I was going to make this friendship last. Mother came and happened to be an old school friend of Mucke's aunt. Mucke's father was German; mine was Polish. She lived in Germany and I in Poland. We were both going to the same seaside resort, at that time a free town surrounded by Poland, but inhabited mainly by Germans. Was this a coincidence, or more than that? I spoke both Polish and German, so the language was no problem.

During the war, in 1940, Mucke came to live in Poland. We saw each other nearly every week and often slept in the same bed. She was a tomboy, always taller than I and my best friend. We saw each other for the last time as children on 13th January 1945, my twelfth birthday. Guns were rumbling in the distance and we knew it was the last time we would see each other in the world as we had known it.

On 17th January 1945 we heard the Russian tanks rolling towards us. Mother and I left with rucksacks on our backs, early in the morning, after I bid a last goodbye to the garden I so loved. Mucke left in a horsedrawn carriage at the same time, but in a different direction I found out many years later.

Eleven years after our last goodbye I met her again. She was a lawyer in Heidelberg and a rather pretty girl with long blonde hair. She was now shorter than I. She had married, but the marriage was obviously on the rocks. It was as though we had never been separated. When I returned to England she came with me. I was doing research for my doctorate, so had plenty of time. She often came to college with me and was very popular there. After eight weeks she returned to Heidelberg. Each of us continued our own life. Her marriage improved and she had two more children. I married my first wife. We saw each other nearly every year. She separated from her husband. I divorced my wife, but we remained the best of friends.

Now twenty-nine years after we had met again, I was driving down to see my "oldest" girlfriend and help celebrate her birthday. She knew I was crazy and would come if she telephoned at the last moment. I knew she was crazy; otherwise, we could not be such good friends.

We did not always agree on social and political matters. She was a little more to the left than I was at the time, but we could discuss any subject, learn from each other and enjoy it. As the years passed we both changed, I perhaps more than she, but we always remained rocks for each other, rocks to which we could cling if we needed to steady ourselves.

Mucke's house was one in which I could relax. Her presence is one which makes life worthwhile. It transcends all other experiences. Why? Do not many of us have such friendships? The answer is now simple to me. From the first moment when I asked to kiss the five-year-old girl's hand, there must have been an energy exchange between us which resulted in a resonance which only we felt, and which was in a subconscious manner pleasing to our souls. There was no sexual desire, just a deep pure love. If one is prepared to believe in past lives, then there must have been a relationship between us, in one or more of them, which we subconsciously remembered when we first saw each other in this life.

Her house must have been pervaded by her energy. Even in her absence I can relax in her lounge as nowhere else. Perhaps the blending of our energies, which some may see as colours, forms a beautiful harmonious shade. She told me how to get into her house in her absence. How often does one have the feeling of well-being, or the opposite, on entering a house, no matter whether that house is comfortable or not, poorly or well furnished, even if one has never met the present occupant?

Whereas I always want to surge ahead and to understand better, Mucke usually accepts situations as they are. So perhaps the energy exchange between us does not result in resonance but a filling in of those parts which the other is lacking. Does it matter which? The two together make each of us feel better. Sometimes it is better to accept than go into reason. This I learned from Mucke, in small doses; every time I met her, a little more. I learned to accept situations and thus gain an inner peace.

The party was glorious and some fifty people were there. The Brazilians were roasting a variety of meats and sausages out in the open. There were plenty of salads, a typical "churrasco", and wine which was flowing freely. I had never been in Brazil so it was all new to me. I certainly had no conscious inkling that I would soon be spending a quarter or more of my life in Brazil.

Many of those who were there I knew but the majority I did not. We were eating out on the lawn. By the time most people had gone home, it was eleven o'clock. A few of Mucke's close friends went up to the living room, a large room in a house built completely of wood. Mucke's taste ran to simple rustic furniture tastefully assembled.

I sat on a settee. Next to me sat a lady I found absolutely fascinating. Out in the garden I had not noticed her. She was a little shorter than I, and slim, with a very expressive mouth, full but not over full beautiful lips, and a small but what appeared to be firm bust not needing a bra. To me this was a woman exuding sex, not of the obvious form, but highly sophisticated and elegant. Her name was Lucia. I had never before been so stunned by a woman in my life. We all chatted until the early morning.

The next day I had to drive back to London. Halfway through

Germany I stopped the car and telephoned Mucke.

"Do you have Lucia's telephone number?"

"No, she moved three days ago and forgot to give me her new number. Why?"

"I am turning back. I must see her again. I have never had a feeling of such intensity."

"You are absolutely crazy. Come back. I shall find her number."

I turned the car round. Mucke had her number. I telephoned.

"Madame, I am Tadeusz, Dr de Gromoboy (we were still on formal terms). It would give me infinite pleasure if you would have lunch with me tomorrow." I was always formal in my initial approaches.

"Oh, yes, I remember you well. Are you not in London?"

"I should be but I felt I had to see you again. Do forgive me, Madame, but I know it is very necessary." I waited for her answer with bated breath.

"Well, yes," her somewhat husky voice replied. "I think I can take some time off for lunch. Collect me at the rehabilitation centre where I work. In the reception area."

My heart was beating fast. This was going to be glorious. Crazy, I know, but glorious. I knew she was an artist. She had just left her husband who had had affairs with other women (the fool to have such a glorious wife and play about with other women). She had sons and worked in the rehabilitation centre because she needed the money. Mucke said she enjoyed the work there though it was only part time; she was good at it.

At 12.00 sharp I was in the reception area. Two minutes later she appeared. I kissed her hand. The charm, the sex and the beauty were all as I remembered them and, most important, the something for which there is no word, something which transcends beauty, charm and intelligence. An attraction resulting from a memory? But what memory? Not one arising from this life. A genetic memory? Or as I now believe a past life memory carried by the spirit inhabiting our present body. She really was pretty, but perhaps not as beautiful as she appeared to me.

How many unattractive men marry beautiful women. Often they are neither wealthy nor have prospects of wealth or importance. Even more surprising, very attractive, wealthy men propose to women who have neither interesting looks nor money. One calls this "chemistry". What is this "chemistry"? It is worth putting a little more thought into it. If we accept the possibility of a memory from a past life the answer would be simple.

We lunched in a restaurant overlooking the river. It was to me a fairy tale lunch. We arranged to meet for dinner and left on first name terms.

In the evening she ate little, but I a lot. We were obviously attracted to each other. I brought her home, kissed her hand and left. I could stay for one more day. It must have been a weekend. We ate lunch with Mucke. In the evening we went out to dinner alone. I brought Lucia home again and could not stop myself when saying goodbye from pressing her to me with my left hand and putting my right under her blouse, gently letting it slide onto her breast. It was a truly magnificent breast, firm and needing no bra to support it. She did not jerk away.

"Now you know a little more about me, do you still like me?"

"Madame, you are magnificent," was all I could answer. I wanted to go further, but I was who I was, an aristocrat as I imagined an aristocrat should be (though I knew that most were not).

"I shall return in two weeks. Will you spend a few days or a weekend with me? Shall we drive to Alsace? The atmosphere there is romantic and the food good."

A moment's hesitation then, "Yes, with pleasure. It's a date. Phone me to confirm exactly when you are coming."

Ten days later I phoned.

"I am still stunned by our encounter. I shall be in Heidelberg in three days. Does our date still stand?"

There was no hesitation this time. "I am looking forward to it."

I spent the night in Mucke's house. The next morning we drove across the border of France into Alsace and a delightful hotel in the country, which I had picked from the Michelin Guide. We both felt great, but after dinner when we went up to our room I felt a little self-conscious.

I had a bath first whilst she undressed. When I finished, I put my dressing gown on and ran a bath for Lucia. She entered the bathroom in her dressing gown. I left politely and closed the door behind me.

Ten minutes later I knocked.

"Come in."

I entered. A most delightful sight hit me. She was a short girl and lay stretched out in the bath with legs slightly separated and breasts firm, as I had imagined, the tips projecting slightly above the surface of the water.

I took my dressing gown off, picked her gently out of the bath, dried her and placed her on the bed. For a time I just stood above her and admired her body. She had the face of a woman not easy to persuade to be made love to; her features were distinct and firm with no smile hovering on the lips, yet something deeply sensuous, a tremendous sex appeal and a distinct gleam in the eyes. All parts of my body stiffened. After two or three minutes her arms stretched out and I came, infinitely slowly, gently, into her. For a moment I did not move, just enjoyed the bliss of being inside this infinitely desirable woman. Then we both began a slow rhythmic motion. The outside world stopped existing.

Later we found ourselves admiring the completely cloudless sky through an open window. We felt no embarrassment; it was as though we had known each other for a long time. Our bodies touched until mine stiffened again and hers softened. This time our motions were more rapid, but after a time my memory blanked out completely. I only remember a feeling of absolute bliss and then exhaustion.

The next morning she remarked, "Your joy was very vocal. I hope we did not awake our neighbours."

"And yours?" I asked.

"I don't remember it fully, but it was great."

The sun began to shine through the window. I took the bedcover off; the lower part of her body was covered with golden light. I kissed her feet, her calves and her thighs, and bliss overcame us again.

After breakfast we drove through the woods, then walked through dense undergrowth, hidden from human eyes, ate somewhere, walked again and enjoyed the beauty of each other and the world. Then we drove until we found another hotel we fancied.

The pleasure we found in each other was no less than during the previous night. We saw castles, forests and ruins; it was an enchanted weekend.

How does one explain these encounters, this tremendous attraction between people, sometimes at first sight and sometimes without a word being spoken, and the absolute knowledge that something will develop, or indeed that nothing will develop in spite of this attraction? Is it an energy that we emanate and which we can receive, rather like radio waves? An energy that tells us something about each other? Tells us about our attraction for each other or indeed about our repulsion for each other? Or is it the memory of an encounter in a past life? Or can it be both? Are we just part of an overall energy reaching from past to future, which is split into different strands, as a prism splits white light into all the colours of the rainbow, with the ability to reunite some strands of the energy, again as prisms can unite different colours to form a third colour, and thus form a pleasing or irritating energy depending on the kinds of energy united?

When I returned to London I wondered whether to feel guilty towards Morena. She liked me in some respects, yet did not want to marry me, and recently had rarely wanted to make love. She seemed to have lost interest in sex - or was it just sex with me?

I felt it might hurt her if I told her. Future events showed that my feelings were right. I would not lie if asked but, if saying nothing would cause the least hurt, then it was best to remain silent.

I flew to Frankfurt frequently. Lucia picked me up at the airport and drove me to her home. We sometimes spent weekends in little inns in the forest. Each time with her was as beautiful as the first.

I experienced some of my most pleasant days to date during this time. I remember glorious breakfasts, which Lucia sometimes prepared and we consumed in bed after our morning shower, or superb crisp rolls which I purchased after our morning exercises and which we ate sitting naked at a beautifully set breakfast table. We both liked elegance and were normally carefully dressed. Lucia had an extremely good dress sense.

Yet it became increasingly obvious that there was probably no future for us. Lucia would not leave her sons to lead their own, most of us thought disastrous, lives. She was their mother. I understood her, yet I felt that by helping them she did not let them express themselves in their own way, even if this way meant that they would be in much trouble. Some people, I felt at the time and still do, need to experience much hardship, as only then will they learn what they have to learn, before they can elevate themselves. If we do not permit them to experience this hardship, we rob them of the experience they are begging for and of the possibility of reaching a higher consciousness.

On 24th July 1986 mother was going to have her 80th birthday. A year earlier her lungs had collapsed and she experienced clinical death, after I had taken her to hospital. She explained to me after she had been resuscitated the feeling of floating and lightness, and the music which she had experienced. She now frequently saw and smelled things which I did not perceive. At the time I thought she was hallucinating and asked a psychiatrist to examine her. I had always loved mother deeply but I did not understand near-death experiences then and the sensitivity which some acquire thereafter.

Though I had also died clinically, I was in a coma afterwards and heavily drugged, so perhaps I forgot if I experienced anything unusual.

I was going to make this birthday for mother a very special one and invite all the people she liked wherever in the world they were.

"I would love to see them all; perhaps it will be the last time. But no, if they are all here, I will be too tired to enjoy them," she said.

"I shall invite them all so that they can see you one or two at a time."

"Who will do the cooking and the cleaning? You will be exhausted. Anyway many of them are old; they will find it difficult to come to London. No, we will just phone them all."

I knew she would love to see them all. Maybe it would be for the last time. She had an oxygen bottle near the bed and another one in the lounge. Even so she frequently could not get enough breath and felt she was suffocating.

Somehow I had to make this a beautiful yet untiring birthday for her. Then it hit me - the obvious answer.

"Mother, I am going to find a hotel, where the air is good, the surroundings beautiful somewhere in the country; yet there will be some shops nearby, but no cars. When you have your good moments you will be able to go out and look at life around you. No noise, no fumes. In central Europe so that it will be easy for all your friends to come, never more than two or three at a time. You will be able to talk about old times and about your children."

"You have always been a dreamer. I am tied to my oxygen bottles."

"There must be some lightweight bottles available. I shall find them. We shall take them with us."

"I am too tired for a long car journey."

"Think about it. We shall talk tomorrow."

"Do you really think I could do it?" she asked the next day. "If I die on the way I shall cause you a lot of trouble."

She was beginning to accept the idea. She might die. So what? It would be better if she died looking forward to something than doing so while sitting bored in an armchair.

"Do you really think you can get lightweight oxygen bottles? But the hotel you describe is a dream; there are no such places in reality."

She had accepted the idea.

I went to our chemist. Yes, he knew a place where they made oxygen in lightweight containers. I drove down to it. Yes, I could hire them. They were light enough for me to lift into my car boot.

Many of mother's friends lived within a 250-mile radius of Heidelberg. I drove down to Mucke and explained my proposal. Did she know any such "dream hotel"? She made one or two suggestions. They were either fully booked or not quite right.

Lucia had a day free. We spent the long weekend driving round the Schwarzwald and Odenwald, both within easy reach of Heidelberg. On the third day we found the ideal place for mother, who does not like the modern noisy hotel, in the market place of an old small town, in the middle of a pedestrian area. There were beautiful views and lovely little boutiques, yet no car noise or fumes. The hotel was small but extremely clean and comfortable; the owner and waitresses were pleasant. It was ideal, and only half an hour's drive from where Lucia lived.

I immediately made reservations - one room for mother and a twin-bedded extra room for guests. A third room could always be found in this hotel or one nearby if necessary, I felt certain.

Then I telephoned all those I thought mother would enjoy seeing. Often it was the children of old friends or relatives. Many of her generation were no longer physically on this earth.

Out of twelve children she was the last one still alive, but there were nephews, nieces, old school friends and college friends, and their children. She, as I and my wife to be, was always a centre trying to keep in touch with everybody she really liked wherever in the world they were.

Mission completed I drove back to London and told her what I had planned. Tears flowed down her cheeks.

"Do you think I will be able to do it? That I will survive the journey?"

At the beginning of July I loaded the car with four oxygen cylinders and a trolley for them, and we started on our trip.

First we went to Mondorf, a village near Bonn, where her favourite brother's son Edmund, usually called Edo by us, and his family lived. When we arrived after an eleven-hour trip, including a relaxing four hours during the Dover to Ostend crossing, she was in better form than she had been for months in London.

Edo and his sister Uta were my favourite cousins. My feelings for them are as great, perhaps greater, than those one has for a brother or sister. We spent the war years 1939 to 1945 together. I have no brothers or sisters.

Once Edo said, or was it Ula his wife, that what they looked forward to most was sitting together when they were old and no longer had any responsibilities. I found and still find this relationship beautiful and in some respects enviable.

As a child Edo, two years older than I, was sometimes quite reckless. I remember he once shot at someone with a catapult from some five metres and hit him in the middle of his forehead; but usually he was quiet and in later years somewhat withdrawn.

During the Second World War we lived in the same compound in Poland, which was under German occupation during the war. The compound consisted of an enormous and beautiful garden, a stocking factory and several houses where my grandparents, some of our relatives and some employees lived. Edo and Uta were the children of my mother's favourite brother, also called Edmund. He considered himself German and worked for Berlin radio, but did not like the Nazis, had difficulties and so joined the army. His wife died and Edo was brought up mainly by Edmund's sister Fritzi whilst Uta was looked after mainly by another sister, Wanda. During the war they were all together in my grandparents' house, and so were my mother and I.

But my mother, having married a Polish officer, rejected her German nationality and both of us had, therefore, no German identity cards. In spite of all pressure, official and private, she refused to consider herself German and brought me up as a Pole. My father had earlier been captured and imprisoned by the Russians. Yet Edo and Uta's father, the German officer, exerted, apart from my mother, the greatest influence on my life. It was he who told me that matter is nearly empty and consisted of atoms quite far apart from each other, each atom consisting of a nucleus surrounded by several electrons, again far away from this nucleus and spinning around it. (I now know that even the electrons and the nucleus are not really matter unless we want to define them as matter. But if we do, then we have to define light, heat, etc. as matter as well.) It was he who looked with me at the stars and wondered who had created them and who, if anybody, lived out there. It was he who made me first wonder what the purpose of life was. It was he who awoke my interest in the scientific method, which I later rejected though this happened well after his death. He was a philosopher and a writer, though he never published any books. He was the sort of person who amasses a tremendous amount of knowledge and could talk about it to those who would listen. My father too thoroughly enjoyed chats with him before the war and again after it, though one was a German officer and the other a Polish one, and both knew that at some time they might be forced to fight each other. Edmund had a tremendous lust for life. Until recently I found it very peculiar that I had also this lust whereas Edo his son did not.

As children we played together and liked each other as brothers, and grew up for four years in each other's company. In 1944 when it was obvious that Germany would lose the war and the Russians overran Poland, Edo, Uta and their aunt Fritzi went to Ernst Junger, a German writer and friend of Edmund, in West Germany. Mother and I could not leave since we were not German and, therefore, could not travel without special permission. When at last the Russians moved into Aleksandrow, the town, now part of Lodz, and where we lived, we withdrew with the front line. In the confusion of war nobody asked for papers, until we reached Kichhorst, a village near Hanover, where Edo and Uta were. There we spent another four months together and enjoyed as children witnessing the spectacular bombing of Hanover. We did not think of the danger or suffering caused, just enjoyed the spectacle, until the Americans occupied this part of Germany.

We knew through the Polish underground that father, after being condemned to death by the Russians, got out of Russia and was in the Second Polish Corps, fighting the Germans under British command. Whereas before we were treated as second-class people, with a ration book allowing two thirds of what the Germans got, we were now the privileged class. The army provided us with chocolate, nuts, cigarettes, etc., which the Germans did not get. Twice a week mother and I walked five miles to the nearest military camp and brought back rucksacks full of goodies.

When father came to collect us we went first to Italy and then England. I graduated in chemistry. Edo trained as a NATO test pilot in the USA and returned to Germany after meeting Ula, his present wife. Uta married a German gynaecologist. Edo enjoyed flying; he must have been good at it since he is still alive. Most German pilots who trained with him died in accidents after their return.

In spite of Edo's romantic background, I became the most adventurous of the three of us and reached reasonable heights in science, with degrees and fellowships in various fields, and travelled all over the world. I still enjoy travel, crossing the Atlantic at least four times every year.

I started talking about and believing in UFOs when I was in my early twenties. Later I became spiritual, not in an orthodox Christian sense, and developed an interest in metaphysical phenomena. Edo and Ula preferred to stay in their home in the country. Edo gets upset with my interest in metaphysics and parapsychology in general since in his opinion anything that cannot be proved "scientifically" must be considered not to exist, whilst Ula believes my interest takes me further away from God. How Ula and Edo can live in the great harmony in which they do live, when one believes that what the other believes is irrational or contrary to God's love, is difficult to understand. Both disagree with my views, one because they are contrary to what many priests say, and the other because much of what I say and believe in cannot be proved "scientifically". Yet we love one another and feel comfortable in each other's company. If any of us should be in need, as has already been the case, the others would do all in their power to help.

Edo is an excellent example of so many people who are good, sincere and helpful in most fields, but will not or cannot believe in some metaphysical aspect. I have shown him films of psychic operations, which I have seen, and brought home parts of human bodies cut out without anaesthetic, but nothing convinced him. I know a highly respected doctor who, after presumably seeing psychic surgery, believed in it, yet later did not. I have understood at last that the whole "spiritual" field is not acceptable to those who have not evolved in a certain way or not yet reached a certain point. Yet one has to talk about it, without insisting. I and many others, who did not understand at one time, understand now. Something opens, sometimes quite suddenly, and much becomes clear. All my previous relationships were beautiful instruments which led me to this opening.

In the West it has perhaps been the Christian Church's fault. Until 869 the human body was believed to consist of body, mind, i.e personality and soul, and spirit. Pope Nicholas then decided that the spirit did not exist and stated that there is only body and mind, and the 8th Ecumenical Council decreed it to be so. It is in this belief that we are brought up, but somewhere inside us the Spirit sits and waits for the curtain to be opened again.

When we entered Edo and Ula's house mother showed a liveliness I had not seen in her for months. We brought in an oxygen bottle, but she waved it away. The next morning she went out into the garden and did a few stretching exercises. My mouth fell open. A healthy body may frequently cause a healthy mind, but a happy and determined mind can certainly cause the body to improve out of all recognition.

Three days later we continued our journey. Mother was chatty all the way. I knew she was going to survive and enjoy her eightieth birthday.

We picked up Lucia and drove the last half-hour to the idyllic hotel. The owner received us with a smile. We brought up her luggage and oxygen containers, explained the type of food mother preferred and that she needed a large table because she would usually have two to six guests, had dinner with her and left her smiling in her room. At the reception we explained again her problems, when to call a doctor, and gave them Mucke's and Lucia's telephone numbers. We left the hotel feeling content in the knowledge that we had done the best we could and that mother was happy.

Perhaps tomorrow she would die. It no longer worried her. She had died before. She wanted to enjoy whatever state she was in. We had talked about it before. This way she felt content, with no secrets from herself or others. I too was learning that at any time now I might no longer be able to talk to her in the same mode as I had during my last forty years. Life is so much more beautiful once one accepts that there is no absolute end. There is a little sadness perhaps just as when a loved one goes for a long time to a different country, but happiness too if one knows that, although he enjoyed being here with his friends, he was looking forward to the new place. Mother was looking forward to her departure.

We returned to Lucia's ground-floor flat. It was small but beautifully and tastefully furnished, with the bedroom window door leading onto a garden at the bottom of which ran a bubbling brook. Our bodies, now free of clothing and all inhibitions, met in joyful exuberance.

The most memorable July for mother and myself had started.

The next morning after our exercises and a shower, followed by a breakfast of fragrant freshly-baked German rolls, thinly sliced Schwarzwualder Schinken, which is a type of dried ham, salami and white cheese, washed down with aromatic coffee, Lucia drove to work and I went to the railway station. The first guest, mother's friend from school, was about to arrive; she was a lady of eighty, now living just two hours by express train from where we now were, together with her daughter Uli and son-in-law Gerd Rabenstain. The praying family I used to call them.

Before every meal a prayer was said. At first I found it a little unusual and embarrassing. It was done with such sincerity and such joy that after the first visit to them I began to look forward to it. I wish we were doing it. There will come a time when we shall.

The next day mother's niece Uta and her husband Klaus Gutting came. Uta, Edo the pilot's sister, was a tiny creature always exquisitely dressed. I loved her deeply. After her mother died, when she was only months old, my parents suggested they would adopt her and bring her up as my sister. She was three months older than I. Her father did not agree, so she was brought up by other maiden aunts.

To me she was a beautiful butterfly, delicately built, perhaps as a ballet dancer or a hostess surrounded by an army of servants with a husband who would adore her, take her to concerts, the opera, the ballet and elegant hotels frequented by high society. She had charm and an excellent dress sense, all admirable characteristics but not for the life of a country gynae-cologist's family. Her house was always perfectly clean; everything was tastefully arranged; the flowers matched the colours of the carpet and the tablecloth, and the food was beautifully served but at what cost. She never complained, but it was obvious to me and my father, who had always liked her deeply, that her body could not take what her spirit demanded of her. She was fragile and often distinctly unwell. Unfortunately few really understood her. She should understand the reality of present life, so many said. Perhaps she should, but not all of us can do what we should do. We are what we are. It is up to all of us to try and understand our fellow human beings, and help them rather than criticise and try to change them, as long as they do no harm.

Uta lived in a fantasy world, a world that no longer existed, a fairy tale world of princes and princesses, yet when necessary could be very realistic. Oh, what a beautiful world, how I would have liked to live in it too. Perhaps that is why I understood her so well. In my middle life I replaced it by sensuousness and spirituality, a peculiar mixture. By sensuousness I mean the appreciation of the beauty, charm and delicacy of the human body. Spirituality to me means the contemplation of matters which go beyond the physical, of realms not fully explicable by contemporary science, a world perhaps not so different from Uta's world at that time. Fortunately I was born with the strength, determination and willingness to use my free will, and not to mind what others thought. I developed the courage to open the window every morning and say in a loud voice, "World, you are beautiful, I love you", just as Uli and Gerd, the praying family, one a business woman and the other a teacher, had the courage to pray out loud or even sing their prayers no matter what company they were in.

Uta was under a continuous stress, even if others could see no reason for it, and as so frequently happens in such cases she suffered from a cancerous growth. When the resistance is low the immune system suffers and cancer flourishes.

When she arrived with her husband Klaus, who loved her deeply and was a good person but like most people could not quite understand her, she looked as ethereally beautiful as ever. Her and Klaus's presence gave mother tremendous pleasure.

Next a college friend of hers arrived, Beate, a remarkable and beautiful woman of mother's age. I and my wife visited her two years ago; she was by then in an old age home but had a boy friend, gave lectures on literary and historical topics, and was clearer in mind and could walk more erect than many a sixty-year-old. This was another example of being what you want to be.

"Old age home, yes, it is comfortable, but I shall not sit back and watch television or knit. I shall read and lecture on what I read, not for money, but for the pleasure of it," she explained to me when I saw her during mother's birthday month.

And so it went on, friends, relatives and children of friends. The weather was perfect, warm but not too hot. Some we brought from and back to the station while others came by car or made their own way. Occasionally we took mother and her guests to visit some local beauty spot or a country restaurant where they served some speciality. An atmosphere of enchanted love and beauty had developed round all of us.

One day I suggested to Lucia, "Let's disappear for a few days."

Somebody suggested an old farmhouse with rustic character and glorious rooms that were, except for a new coat of paint and a bathroom, as they had been two hundred years ago - and superb food we were told. We bought a few bottles of good wine, one of champagne for our arrival and a good liqueur for when we felt particularly "sweet", and drove into the middle of the Black Forest where our haven was. We got the room we asked for; it was a hut standing alone surrounded by flowers. We opened the door to find white walls, brown crooked beams, a ceiling slanting steeply on two sides, old-fashioned wooden furniture, the window facing the wood and an enormous double bed. Somewhat incongruously there was a large brown deep carpet. At the side of the entrance hall was a door leading to a modern bathroom tiled and with an enormous mirror.

We took our clothes off and Lucia went to have a shower. I uncovered the bed, placed the bottles of wine on the dressing table - what the maid would think did not worry me and opened the champagne.

When I heard the hair dryer running I knocked on the bathroom door.

"Come in."

I entered with two glasses in my hands and saw her body from behind, and her face and breasts reflected in the mirror.

"What, now?" she asked. "My hair is still wet."

"No, no! First the champagne."

It was easier to say "No, no", than to act it. My body showed clearly that the "no" was only a word, but we did drink our wine first. I do not remember the taste.

The room was pervaded by evening sunlight. She walked slowly with a majestic step towards the bed and lay flat on it, this time smiling at me, her slightly wet hair glistening at the side of her face. Like the first time, nearly a year ago, I stood there transfixed by the charm and invitation of her body, before I covered every spot on it with kisses and then she whispered, "Come." I entered.

I know we had dinner, because I remember when returning admiring the clear sky with its stars and a bright moon, but the details are blurred.

When we returned, mother merely remarked, "You look radiant."

I felt it. I might have been fifty-three but I felt in my early twenties.

For the rest of the month we went nearly every day to mother and certainly met everybody who visited her, at least fifty people from all over Europe. She was never tired, used only half as much oxygen as I thought she would and was always radiant. Everybody who left said they had learned something from her. It must have been the enlivening happy energy she was radiating. Then I could only guess at it. Now I know it. A few days ago I saw this energy for the first time - not mother's, as she is no longer in the flesh. My wife has been seeing some of it for many years. I feel certain we are entering an era when more and more people will see the energy we emit and how it varies depending on our state of mind. Already very few can see the interplay of energy between people when they converse, argue or feel an attraction for each other. Kirlian photography can show, under controlled conditions, that the energy emitted by a healer is different when he is in a passive condition and whilst he is actively healing.

We frequently went with Lucia for walks in the country or through the forest. Sometimes I experienced a feeling as though I was nearly floating and life on the earth was not quite real, and that there was another life in which my physical body was not the only body that mattered, nor my only real body. Sometimes I also experienced this feeling when in the large sitting room of Mucke's wooden house. Then I did not talk about it. It seemed absurd. I now feel that I exist on several levels and, when in the right mood and helped by the right energy surrounding me, can move my consciousness from one level to another. I now freely admit it and have found that I am not the only one to have such experiences.

Sometimes when Lucia went to work I sat in her garden, listening to the bubbling brook, reading a book or just staring at the clouds. Again I sometimes felt I was leaving the reality I was accustomed to and for moments entering another world, which in a way was part of this world.

Caro, Mucke's daughter, often visited mother. She felt particularly elated after each visit. She had a special relationship with her. Why does one person so frequently have a special effect on another?

It was an enchanting time only to be repeated years later when I was beginning to be conscious of what was happening to me. Mother was in an equally glorious mood, smiling, entertaining and hardly ever out of breath.

On our way back to London we stopped again to see Edo and Uta, and then in Belgium to visit Agi and her husband Herbert. Agi was the youngest daughter of another of mother's school friends, whose husband was once a great admirer of my mother. After the war, by hard work and commercial intuition, they became wealthy again, built a factory and were highly recognised citizens of Wilhelmshaven where they had settled. Agi went to a ladies' finishing school in England but, when she returned home, fell in love with her riding teacher, the son of a simple farmer-butcher. Both parents were unhappy about the relationship. His because Agi was unable to do any of the simple household chores they considered a wife of their son ought to be able to do. Hers because he was below their station in social life. They trusted me and asked me to visit them and persuade their daughter to change her mind. I met Herbert, a tall handsome man, who spoke well and in my opinion knew better how to behave than many from high society do. I liked him and was not prepared to interfere. Are we ever allowed to interfere in these matters?

Since neither of the parents were happy about their children's relationship, the two left their home town, went to Belgium and started making sausages by hand which they sold in the market. Agi, the girl who could not wash dishes when with her parents, could do anything when with the man she loved. They first built a small factory, then a larger one and then a very large one, and exported meat products all over the world. Since 1970 both he and I were beginning to become really wealthy. We saw each other frequently. He had two daughters and I had two sons. What I admired about him was that he never showed off his wealth. He liked riding, so he bought good horses and built a beautiful stable, but never talked of money or tried to impress. For a long time he and Agi were very happy. To me both seemed well-rounded people. Neither relied on the other and they co-operated because they wished to do so. Each set of their parents changed their attitude, liked and admired and fully trusted their child-in-law.

When my mother and I visited them on our way back there was something distinctly wrong, though both were smiling and hospitable as always.

"Come with me, Tadek, I have to buy something in town," Herbert said.

In the car he reached into his pocket and took out a photograph.

"Look at her. Is she not a beauty?"

"Yes, who is she?"

"A woman I love. What do you think I should do?"

"Wait," I said. "Find out how deep your feelings really are."

I knew his wife was only a little younger than he; this lady looked much younger. I knew that men often had to have a "fling" and it usually passed. But was it only men? My wife had left me. I knew how much disruption it could cause. I liked Agi; she was a good-looking and extremely capable woman.

All I could say was, "In many ways I understand. Enjoy your flirtation, but do not let anybody know. The feeling may pass and you do have a deep and well-established relationship with Agi."

When we returned to his house, it soon became obvious that Agi not only suspected but knew. Later he broke off the relationship with the girl whose photograph he had shown me, but started one with another girl. He was not a flirt in the obvious sense. In his, as in so many cases today, he was no longer satisfied with what he had achieved or the type of life he had led. He was trying to find himself. He first thought of expanding his production to Ireland, then even Australia, but in the end sold his factory. Agi and Herbert were both good people; they were never trying to use or dominate each other for they were both too well rounded. Often such a relationship can lead to a lifelong co-operation. Sometimes when each has learned from the other what they needed, they separate. Perhaps that is the way it was meant to be. It should never be done without deep thought.

Even in Christianity it is only the Roman Catholic Church which does not recognise divorce at all. A divorced person cannot remarry in the Church. But the Roman Catholic church does recognise a marriage in the

Orthodox Church so a divorced Roman Catholic who remarries in the Orthodox Church is recognised as being married by the Roman Catholic Church. All a little confusing.

It is only within our conscience that we know what is right and wrong. Our conscience is part of the whole cosmic consciousness. Others frequently tell us what is right or wrong. Often they do so because they wish to exert a power over us, so that they can profit by it.

We are now at a stage where many of us know our own abilities and are no longer prepared to be led blindly by others. All we can do is lovingly advise and gently suggest. The individual must decide. If force is used, whether by politicians or the church, the results are invariably opposite to those they hope to achieve. For confirmation we need only look at the recent collapse of communism, which as an ideal had many positive aspects, but the methods of enforcement were pure brutality; the crime rate and youth gangs in America which the police with its often indiscriminate and forceful methods is unable to control, and the emptying Roman Catholic churches, in spite of the fact that the priests no longer loudly proclaim that only Catholics can go to heaven.

CHAPTER 6

World You Are Beautiful, I Love You
To remember can be the greatest gift.

In September 1987 father's Brazilian school friend, who was now a Brazilian national, and his truly Brazilian wife were visiting us again. Cysinka said, talking of Elizabeth her ex-pupil who had spent a weekend in my house nine years ago, "She still remembers and talks of you." The second statement was not true, so Elizabeth told me later. "You must come and visit us." They had been inviting me for the last fifteen years, yet I had never gone to Brazil.

My memory sprang into action. Was it only the memory of nine years ago?

I wrote another letter to Elizabeth, telling her what I was doing now, what my hopes were and that I would like to have a companion for life again. Effectively it was another marriage proposal, but I did not mention to her that I no longer remembered her face. I told the Blochs, my parents' friends, that this time I would certainly come to Brazil and visit them.

After their return Elizabeth showed them my letter to her and asked, "Is your friend crazy?"

"No, Elizabeth, not crazy. He is Polish."

It was true that my parents were Polish; perhaps there is not much difference between a Pole and a crazy person. Both can be idealists.

After my letter to Elizabeth I phoned her to make sure she would be in São Paulo when I arrived, and bought a flight passage. I knew I was going to marry the girl. It was not a completely conscious knowledge. It was on the edge of consciousness.

On 12th October 1987 1 arrived in São Paulo. Richard de Bloch met me at the plane with a friend of his, the ex-chief of the airport police. I think he brought him so that I would not have to stand in any queues and could be whisked straight to a waiting car after picking up my luggage. In

Richard's home his wife and Elizabeth received me with smiling faces and Brazilian hospitality. The Blochs lived in a beautiful flat, elegantly furnished with a fine library.

To my astonishment and pleasure I was told that I was going to sleep in Elizabeth's parents' house. Why I had no idea and Elizabeth had even less so; she was simply asked whether she and her parents would put me up. The Blochs had no idea about my feelings and premonition in respect of Elizabeth. We never understood why they had done this. Since Elizabeth had spent a few days in my house and her parents, the Restainos, were a very hospitable family as I found out later, they agreed that I could stay in their home.

Elizabeth drove us to her flat. Her mother had prepared an excellent lunch, excellent because she always prepared excellent food, particularly when they had guests; but I remember nothing of it except Elizabeth next to whom I was seated. I could not keep my eyes away from her. This was the woman I was going to spend the rest of my life with.

The next day she asked me to sit next to her on an armchair in the lounge.

"You look at me as a woman. I look at you as a friend of friends. I shall show you the sights of São Paulo, the countryside, and the mountains nearby where my sister lives. I shall take you to our flat at the seaside, but that is all."

"Thank you, but life is not too long. Should we not make full use of all the beautiful moments it provides?"

"I know what you mean. I have heard this often before. It is not that you are not handsome nor that you are nineteen years older than I. No, it is just that you are to me only a friend of my friend. Can we leave it at that?"

I knew better than to argue. Elizabeth was a determined woman who knew her mind. She had graduated in tourism and then taken a postgraduate degree in business administration, but decided that neither was what she would dedicate her life to. She had always dreamt about travelling and seeing much of the world, but not as a career. She had undergone thirteen operations to make her left leg, which had been disabled by polio, usable, and knew one of the top plastic surgeons in Brazil. She asked him if she could watch an operation, but this time not as a patient, and then

74

asked him to train her as a theatre nurse. She had no nursing experience, but in Brazil anything is possible with the right contacts. This is what she wanted to do, and she did it excellently. Later she trained new assistants and her surgeon used to say that, if she but had a licence, she could perform the operations herself.

It was always her dream to spend some time in England, so she wrote to Cambridge, arranged to be enrolled in the course of her choice and asked the college to find accommodation for her close to her place of study since she had a leg problem. Only then did she tell her parents who had always in the past found good reasons why she should not go now - a wedding or a christening. They probably did not want her to go because they were afraid of the problems she might have, especially as she had only one usable leg. So she told them at the last moment that everything was arranged, and she was about to start packing. She was a determined girl or, as I liked to think, she knew that I was in England and that the time had come for her to meet me. This was in 1978. It was then that we met for the first time. Obviously neither of us were quite ready for each other, so when we did meet we did not know the purpose of our meeting.

Now in 1987, I knew the time had come. I kissed her hand and said, "All right, whatever you say I shall adhere to. That does not mean that I accept it as your final decision."

It all sounded a little peculiar to me. I mean my own words and my own feelings. It was all quite irrational. I had not yet learned to accept intuitive feelings, though I had begun to realise that they were to be taken into account. After all, my letters to Elizabeth and my flight to Brazil were both irrational. I was living in a dream, but I lived it. The world was beautiful.

São Paulo was the most peculiar town I had seen. Its population was probably about fourteen million. It had doubled during the last twenty years. There were some beautiful colonial-style houses left, but during the last twenty years whenever one was for sale a skyscraper was built in its place. They did not even stand parallel to each other, but were built to use all the area available. Today one might buy an apartment on say the 10th floor with a reasonable view from its windows. Next month another skyscraper might be built and all one could see from the windows would be a wall and other windows. Planning authorities existed, so I was told, but a few thousand dollars into the right pockets would get permission to build anything a developer thought profitable. Sometimes one saw a small house sandwiched between two or three skyscrapers with practically no light reaching it. Yet on the whole the city has its charm once one gets used to it.

The roads are wide, some lined with trees, but a local authority may decide to cut down the trees to make room for a bus lane. Many wide new roads have been built, especially along the river which goes in a "U" shape through the town, and the traffic flows no worse than in other large towns, except when it rains. The gutters cannot take the water from the fairly frequent tropical downpours, and for a few hours havoc reigns with one or more feet of water causing the road surface to vanish. All houses have garages. In skyscrapers one or two underground floors are used as parking places. The ground floor is always arranged as an area for reception, which any tenant can use. Most have swimming pools. For the middle and upper classes life is comfortable. All families have at least one maid, often two. Some have a driver as well to take the children to school and deliver items to friends.

Many live in shanty towns which spring up along canals and motor-ways, and on hilly ground on which it is too difficult to build skyscrapers economically. Sometimes, I am told, they spring up in people's back gardens when they are away. Some live under bridges or just nowhere.

Traffic lights are mainly there for decoration. I once heard the police advise not to stop at red lights at night, particularly in some parts of town, because of the danger of being assaulted. One does not go for walks in town; it is too dangerous. I have never taken it very seriously, but I suppose there is much truth in it since everybody I know has been assaulted or had something stolen from them at least once, some several times.

A short time ago my father-in-law drove out to buy some fruit. He likes to choose his own. Two gentlemen walked up to him, produced a gun and said, "Old man, your car keys." He handed them over.

"Your wallet." He handed it over.

"But at least give me some money so that I can get a taxi and take my fruit home."

They opened his wallet and gave him enough for a taxi.

Others were not so lucky. When somebody who looked like a young beggar asked some friends of ours, sitting in a car with their baby son, for some money and did not get it, he pretended to stroke the baby and cut its jugular with a razor blade. Our car was broken into five times, during a particularly unlucky year, within the three months we spent in São Paulo. All this may be true yet somehow I do not feel threatened when in Brazil. The people are pleasant and very hospitable. They are never on time and this is something that will have to change before Brazil will become the most important country in the world, which I feel certain will be the case in the near future.

Elizabeth drove me to Campos do Jordao, a town built in the mountains where the houses are all in a neo-Tirolean style - a peculiar feeling to see Alpine houses in Latin American tropics. There among the steeproofed houses I had the first indication that Elizabeth was beginning to realise what would happen between us. Then she took me to Guaruja, the middle-class seaside resort of São Paulo, where I swam for the first time in the South Atlantic.

Guaruja - never in my life have I felt so good, so pampered and so honoured. It was a tropical spring. The sun shone continuously without being too hot. Every desire Elizabeth felt that I might have she fulfilled. On the beach she bought me fresh fruit juice, ice creams and freshly picked oysters which for the first time in my life I really enjoyed. She took me to the best fish restaurant I have ever been to. She bought me caipirinha, a typical Brazilian cocktail, though she never drinks alcohol. For the first time I felt that someone, who owed me nothing, tried to give me everything. It probably happened before, but I never perceived it with such intensity - again a question of the right energy interplay. It was there that I told her that when she came to England she would be my queen. She is my queen in every sense, and yet my friend and equal.

The difference between our relationship and any other I had had before was that neither of us needed the other, but both of us felt good giving to the other. Without any reason, with nothing in our conscious past being responsible for it, both of us enjoyed the getting, but enjoyed even more the giving. This has never changed. It is the only form of relationship and energy interplay that can lead to an everlasting love. It is undemanding yet grateful.

Then Richard's son-in-law drove me and his wife to Rio de Janeiro where he lived. The beaches there are visually beautiful, but the sea waves are so powerful that it is difficult to get into the water. I found this every time I went there. The old beautiful houses along the beaches and the roads running parallel to the beach have been replaced by enormous tall buildings, though a law has been passed not permitting new construction of more than twelve stories. To me it is a town built exclusively for tourists, at least along the beach. Many like it and some hate it. Parts, far behind the beaches reaching into the hills and national parks, are glorious. Few tourists go there, in spite of the large and often colourful houses amongst luscious vegetation which is a feast for the eye.

As in São Paulo, shanty towns have sprung up wherever a piece of land was unused. During the day, beggars are in evidence everywhere; at night people sleep on pavements next to elegant hotels and restaurants, a mixture of modern elegance with abject poverty. It is not a town I would choose to live in, in spite of some remarkably beautiful spots, buildings and views such as the new cathedral and the view from the Christ statue, a thousand feet above the town and a symbol visible for miles.

Some feel the atmosphere there to be depressing and avoid the town if they can. Others come from far and wide and love it.

In spite of all the corruption and poverty I saw, my feeling that Brazil would become extremely important, in a positive sense, within fifteen years deepened.

Why I felt this certainty I had no idea. I knew little about intuition. It confused me. Now I know that these "intuitive feelings" have to be taken seriously. In my case and in that of many others, they have usually become a reality - not always. We have a free will which can change the probabilities which we feel intuitively.

From Rio de Janeiro I flew to the capital Brasilia, some six hundred miles inland. Richard had arranged for me to be met by a highly-placed civil servant to give me an idea of the political life; also an editor of a newspaper, and a professor at the Brasilia University since I wanted to know what it looked like and what its standards were.

I found the town fascinating. Built in the middle of a desert in 1960 it gave me the impression of literally another world. Constructed in the shape of an aeroplane, the main roads are six lanes wide and the main government buildings are where the cockpit would be. The houses of parliament are like mushrooms, one being upside down. There are H-shaped, Z-shaped and cone-shaped buildings and the cathedral is built of glass. Every block has its own infant school and supermarket. There is practically no public transport. Everybody seems to have a car, but there is little traffic on the roads. The houses are low and most have their own swimming pool; I saw none without. At first only government employees lived there and, of course, shopkeepers and restaurateurs to cater for them. Many said it was a city without a soul. I did not find it so. By the time I visited it, over twenty years after it had been built, many retired government officials, who were expected to leave after their term of office was over, decided to stay there. Satellite towns had to be built. I was shown all the sights in a special VIP glass-covered van with my own driver and a guide whose special pass opened all doors.

Perhaps this was not the most natural way of seeing a town, but it added to the impression of being in another world.

From there I went another 1500 miles north to Manaus in the middle of the jungle, on the banks of the Amazon river which is a mile or more wide with white sandy beaches along its banks. I spent a day walking through and sleeping in the jungle with an Indian guide and a barman-cook all to myself for only US $100. Again it was a little artificial, but if one does not know the jungle, an experience not to be missed. The jungle sounds at night, and swimming in the river with what I was told were vegetarian crocodiles, all added to a heightened perception of nature.

From there I was supposed to fly back to Rio de Janeiro and London - but how could I? Elizabeth was really all that mattered to me. We had experienced one moment when I realised that she might in the end - no, I really knew she would - marry me. So I flew back to São Paulo instead, and spent a few more days with her before returning to London.

In Brazil everything is possible if you have the right contacts. Richard did. The last thing in his life that he did for me was to make my return journey a luxurious one. I had to fly via Rio. There a hostess called me, took my ticket away and handed me another one - first class. He had asked for me to be upgraded. In my mind it was more than an upgrading of an air ticket. My life had been upgraded. Through him I met Elizabeth. Elizabeth was the cause of my biggest step, one to a higher level of consciousness.

I spent the night flight in complete luxury, thinking about life and its purpose, writing a long letter to Richard and making sure, by believing without permitting any doubt to enter my mind, that Elizabeth would soon come to England and a life of bliss would start for us.

Morena I loved because she had a charm and youth which I admired and needed. Need is not the best reason for a lasting relationship. It leads to addiction which in any form is not good. Lucia was a glorious experience, one of the type which is healthy, enriches life and shows one what is possible, yet at the same time is one which is meant to be temporary; to hold on to it would spoil the beautiful memories it leaves.

Elizabeth was different. I did not need her. She did not need me. But I knew that the rest of our life was meant to be spent together. In our individual fullness we could make each other's fullness even greater. We each were an "O", a complete circle. The two "Os" together gave the symbol for infinity, . An infinite depth of understanding and an endless flow of energy, including the continuous flow of love and emotion, could develop. All my previous relationships were instruments which led me to this appreciation. One should always consider what an event in life teaches one. We did not have to demand anything from each other. We could freely give if we wanted to. By the time the plane landed at Heathrow I knew what the future would be. I was in a semi-trance yet fully in reality.

This was a state which I was to experience frequently in the future, one which I now know most of us can experience if we want to. All we have to do is relax completely and let thoughts come to us without forcing them, above all believing that what will come to us is good not only for us and our friends, but also in an absolute sense. I believe it to be good if we feel ourselves enveloped by a white light, though recently I often prefer a golden light. The most difficult part is to suspend all doubt, if one has an orthodox or scientific upbringing as I have, and not to think that one is crazy. Once one has said one or two things which one knows nothing about, but which turn out to be facts happening elsewhere or events which occur in the near future, it becomes much easier to believe that one is connecting to an all-pervasive energy.

I telephoned Elizabeth every day. I could not help myself. It was not a feeling of an obsessive necessity, but one of it being the natural thing to do.

On February 3rd 1988, she came to London. I believe she knew it was what she had to do, but she said at the time that it was to find out what this peculiar person who phoned her every day was like in his own surroundings. When I saw her at Terminal 4 of Heathrow airport, it was as if the lights became brighter.

We spent a month travelling all over central Europe. I wanted to show her the things I liked and also to introduce her to my friends and relatives who lived all over Europe.

I told her that I knew a little about healing and was beginning to take an interest in esoteric fields. We talked very little about it. She just told me that she too was interested in these fields and had been for many years.

It was a glorious time. We had decided nothing about ourselves, except that she would come again.

"No or little travelling this time," she said.

"I want to see what normal life in your house is like," she added.

"Whatever you say, but come soon."

At the airport she bought me Shirley MacLaine's book *Out on a Limb*.

"Read it. I think you need it."

I did not know anything about film stars, even less about esoteric writers. She gave me no idea what the book was about. I was not looking forward to reading it. I gathered it was biographical. I was not interested in biographies of film stars.

After a few pages it gripped me. It introduced me to happenings which were impossible, yet the way she wrote about them convinced me that they were reality. I found a scene describing someone "channelling", i.e. speaking in an altered voice, with words and ideas which were apparently not his own but those of another "entity". It was absolutely fascinating. I wished I could meet somebody who had this ability.

A few days later I met Janine at one of the healing sessions conducted by Philippa. I told her I was interested in importing leather goods from Poland. She told me her father had been in this field and could give me some hints. She arranged for me to meet him. When I arrived at her parents' house, her mother, Beatrice, received me. She was a charming lady of Dutch origin. We talked and talked. Her husband did not arrive.

I do not know why, but at some stage I said, "I have read something about channelling. Have you ever heard of it? I would love to meet someone who has this ability."

"Would you really? Do you think you are ready for it?"

Oh! She obviously knew something about it.

"I do not know, but I sure would like to experience it."

"Come next week to this place," she said giving me an address. "Ursula Roberts, the best medium I know, will give a channelled lecture there."

This was going to happen with increasing frequency; if I wanted or needed something to happen it would, often in completely unexpected ways. Later I learned to "pray" for it. If it was right for me, it would happen.

When Ursula appeared she was obviously in a trance; I say obviously even though I had never seen anybody in a trance before. Her eyes had an "unfocussed" look which is the only way I can describe it.

She spoke of a "summer land" where spirits, or some spirits, went to after the body died. They "lived" there in a "make believe" (my word) land. If they wanted to live in a large house in the country, they would imagine it and live there. If they wanted a river to flow through the back garden, there would be one. This was all fascinating but difficult to accept.

Beatrice had arrived after me, but sat next to me. At one stage my throat became dry and I started coughing. She handed me a boiled sweet.

"Do not worry. It nearly always happens when you first experience Ursula channelling."

When the lecture finished the voice that was hers and yet not hers, and which had a peculiar accent even though I had been told that Ursula was English, asked for questions. They came.

"There is somebody here who has not been here before. Does he not have any questions?"

I did not think it was referring to me. No questions came. The voice repeated its request so I asked, "I know nothing about the matters you have talked about, but recently I found that I developed an interest in them. Why?"

"Because you are ready for it. There is someone next to me who says he is your father. It is he who told me to talk about the matters I talked about. He says you need that knowledge."

It was all a little confusing. Why was it not father's voice that spoke?

Chapter 6

I did not argue. Father had died many years ago and never showed any interest in esoteric matters. If it was really father's spirit, why did he not speak to me directly?

When I returned home I told mother what had happened. There was also a friend in the house.

"Can you smell it?" mother said.

I was going to ask, "What?" But then it hit me. If I had doubts before, they were smaller now. I looked at our friend. She nodded.

"Yes," she said.

"Yes," I repeated.

It was the intense aroma of Erimore Mixture which father used to smoke in his pipe. We were silent for a little while. It was a new experience for all three of us. Did we imagine it, because I had mentioned father?

In the future I was to experience smells which were typical of people. Until I was told, I did not know it appeared whenever their "spirit" was "near". What does "near" mean in "spiritual" terms? Now I think I know. All that some spirits are able to manifest, which is perceptible by everybody, is a smell. If they wish a person or a group to know that they exist and are observing them for whatever reason, they may manifest a smell which those who know them or know of them will recognise.

Just before Elizabeth had returned to Brazil, Philippa telephoned and told me that Lilla, a medium, would like to talk to me. I had met Lilla once but did not know she was a medium. I went to see her after Elizabeth's return to Brazil.

I did not know what to expect. Except for Ursula, whom I had seen whilst in a trance, I had never knowingly met a medium before. Would smoke come out of her ears when she spoke or would it be from the nose?

She was a charming lady of Polish origin and my age. We spoke first about various matters such as where she lived and when she had come to England; both of us had done so when we were children. Then we got down to business. She looked at me, said she could see colours centring on some parts of my body and spoke in a completely normal voice, answering questions if I did not understand something. When I asked her how she knew so much about me, she answered that it just came to her. She told me that I was a healer, but might not like to heal in the ordinary way. I healed by speaking to people and looking at them. If I wished to I could, yes I probably would, lead and organise ... she hesitated ... healers and people working in this field. I might organise a healing centre. My work in the past was a preparation for my more important activity - to do what I promised to do whilst I was still a spirit.

It was difficult but somehow acceptable. I did believe in a God, so a spirit seemed a natural consequence.

"Elizabeth and you have been together before. Things often went wrong. You promised each other that next time, if only possible, you would meet again. You had to meet. This time everything will be good for you. Yes, the probability is that everything will be perfect. You are the best thing that could happen to her and she the best thing that could happen to you."

The tape recorder was running. I had not imagined her words. I was delighted, but the implications were difficult to swallow. It meant reincarnation. I knew the dictionary's definition of the word, but emotionally it was something that happened to Indians when they changed into cows.

Since then I have thought much about reincarnation and have come to the conclusion on the basis of what I read and experienced that either reincarnation exists or there is a cosmic computer which has all knowledge of what happened in the past. If the latter was the case then some of us have a smaller, and others a greater, facility to plug into this computer or perhaps both reincarnation and the cosmic computer exist.

It is a proven and well-documented fact that some children, before they have been indoctrinated as to what is "possible" or "impossible", speak of that which they did before or describe past events. Some adults can do this too and many can be "regressed" under hypnosis. In one case a friend of mine regressed a person who then described a scene in a pub in which he said he was sitting. He mentioned the name of the pub and the village in which it was. Through the window, he said, he saw three trees and described them. The pub existed in the village he mentioned, but there was only one tree of the type he mentioned as being visible through the window. This was one of the many cases where the evidence was inconclusive, until by chance somebody said that about forty years ago two trees which stood close to the existing one were cut down. To me the evidence for reincarnation is now fairly conclusive, although a "cosmic computer" might also be a possible explanation. There are other bits of information, including the fact that many religions accept reincarnation as a certainty.

The fact that two years after I had met Elizabeth for just a day or two, I suddenly remembered her and had an intense desire to marry her, though I knew nothing about the girl, and that another seven years later the same thing happened again, though this time I did not even remember what she looked like, is to me best explained by assuming that we either met as spirits or in previous lives or both. That I remembered her only occasionally is no different to what happens to memories from within this life. They suddenly come and one does not know why, and then they go again. In that particular case there are of course other possible explanations, such as a genetic memory or telepathy. But we come from different parts of the world, and she said she never thought of me, except when she received the two letters from me, one two years and the other nine years after we met.

Lilla also told me that, "Elizabeth can see colours."

"So can I and most people," I answered.

"No," she said, "she can see colours round people. She can see auras and she can heal people using colours."

I sent a copy of the tape to Elizabeth, by now in Brazil, and asked her what this meant.

"Yes," she answered, "I sometimes do see colours round people. I know some can do it whenever they want to. To me it happens just sometimes. The first time it happened it frightened me terribly. I thought I was going mad."

When she feels that someone is ill or nervous or has to take an examination she will tell him to imagine himself enveloped in a given colour. She may also put a photograph or the name of a person under a colour filter and place them on the window shelf, with the sun shining onto it. Some people ask her to put their name into her "colour box" and claim that it helps them to overcome a difficulty or pass an examination. There is no proof, of course, but just a feeling they have.

At one stage Lilla gazed at my stomach or lower area. I looked at her smiling.

"What are you looking at?"

"It is your colour there that interests me. It is going to rise." Her gaze went up. "Oh yes, if you want to you can do it. You have all the possibilities."

Reincarnation I had come across before; difficult as its acceptance might be, it did not shake me as much as these colours did which she saw on various parts of my body. They had a meaning to her and they also served as a focus to permit ideas to come to her from "somewhere" and which she verbalised whilst looking at my "colours".

Since then I read a little about this. Apparently there are several energy centres within our body which are able both to pick up energy from the outside and emit energy which some people can see. These centres are called chakras.

There are seven main chakras in our body. Named differently by various schools of thought, one is centred near the bottom of the trunk, usually called the base chakra and seen as red in colour by some, and is said to absorb energy from the earth and pass it on to the higher chakras. Next up is the second chakra, also given various names; I call it the digestive chakra; in my present opinion, it is not only responsible for sexual energy as some think, but also for transmuting energy from various sources into the type of energy needed by the various parts of the human body. It is seen by some as having an orange colour. Above this at the height of the navel is the solar plexus, yellow, and said to be responsible for providing healing energy for the physical body. Above this is the fourth chakra, known as the heart chakra, green in colour, and associated with love. In the opinion of many, it is the most important chakra for the complete functioning of the human being from both the spiritual and physical point of view. The fifth is the throat chakra, light blue in colour and responsible for communication on a physical level. In the centre of the forehead is the sixth chakra, also know as the third eye, dark blue in colour. It facilitates communication on a higher level, such as by telepathy and with other spirits. The seventh and last chakra is the crown chakra, violet in colour and responsible for contact with our higher self and the highest level in general. For a full and healthy life, all chakras should be equally developed and in line.

I listened to her tape again just now, seven years later. She also said then that my sense of values would change and within five years I would move to a different level. This part I had forgotten. She was right. My financial position has stopped being important to me. I see people in a different way, do not judge them and accept that they are what they are. If they are from many others' point of view "peculiar" perhaps they need to be so to experience something that is required for their full development. Perhaps, of course, they are using their free will wrongly. I may say something to make them think about their actions and their mode of behaviour, but I will never insist. The decision must be theirs.

Six, not five, years passed when I quite suddenly knew that I was about to "know" things which by normal physical means I could not "know", and that I would channel or, as I prefer to call it, connect with the "all-pervasive energy" or "joint consciousness".

Perhaps the most significant point Lilla made, which I had forgotten, was that my feeling for Elizabeth was one of affinity, which is much more than love, surpasses all other feelings and is lasting.

Sure, I felt a sexual attraction for her. I loved every part of her body. I found it difficult to keep my hands away from her small but firm bust. I could look at her beautiful smile for ever. Making love to her was a new dimension. Even her deformed leg was to me attractive. I could sit holding her hand and find the most beautiful shiver going through my body, not far removed from feeling an orgasm yet in a way that was spiritual. But however exciting her presence and her body were, there was a feeling of calmness and permanence superimposed on the atmosphere which I knew was enveloping us. It is this atmosphere which gives depth to a relationship. It does not result from a physical attraction, but from a mixing of energies which people emit. This mixture may result in a more or less pleasant atmosphere. Indeed it is this mixture which determines not only the atmosphere in which people live, but also that which they radiate to others. An atmosphere which may be pleasant or abrasive.

CHAPTER 7

Encountering the Impossible
Nothing is impossible, only to us it may seem inexplicable.

Two months after Elizabeth left for Brazil she returned to England. It was May. England was a garden of flowers. My heart was beating a little more rapidly. My lusty eyes were not looking on the beautiful scantily dressed figures of women in spring. I had always found the opposite sex even more attractive at this time of the year. Nature was ripening. What is there that is more beautiful than the ripening body of a female whatever her age? An expectancy shows in her movements, in the way she holds her body, and in the thoughts and desires that pass between people.

This May, as in all the Mays to come, my excitement was devoted to Elizabeth.

Just before she was to come, several friends from abroad telephoned and asked whether they could come and stay in our house. I had always said yes and did so now. There was Evelyn from China and her daughter Kathryn who spend some time every summer in my house; there was Lucia from Germany, my last girlfriend, and her son; there was Ernst, an Austrian friend of mine whom I had known for some twenty-five years, with his son, and one or two others I cannot remember. My mother, usually an extremely hospitable woman, was horrified.

"You want to marry Elizabeth. When she comes and sees a mixture from the whole world in what you hope will be her house, she will realise you are truly mad. At this stage you are supposed to devote all your time to her."

"Is it not better if she knows now what I am really like, that this is my life?"

"Hm, well, I can only pray for you."

When I collected Elizabeth from the airport I told her that the house was full of, for her, strangers including my last girlfriend.

"How lovely," was her answer. "Just as in my house in Brazil - always more guests than we can really put up."

It turned out to be one of the most beautiful fortnights I had experienced. The sun shone every day. We all ate breakfast together in the garden, accompanied by the songs of birds. Then most of the guests went sightseeing, while one stayed behind to help prepare dinner. In the evening we all had our meal in the garden again, this time accompanied by the sounds of soft music. Local friends visited often and at times there were as many as fourteen of us. It was a fairy tale atmosphere never to be forgotten.

On the second day this time round in London Elizabeth said, "You know I cannot cook."

"Yes, you told me." I assumed she could not prepare complicated dishes.

"I don't know how to boil rice or potatoes."

"Don't worry. I know how it is done."

Of course she was exaggerating. Everybody knew how to boil potatoes. The proof came in minutes. We had cleaned some vegetables which were to be boiled and Elizabeth started preparing a raw salad. She could certainly do that. I went out into the garden to cut some flowers.

"The buzzer on the cooker is ringing. What do I do?"

"The potatoes are ready. Turn them off."

I continued doing something in the garden. I knew she was still preparing the salad and setting the table. When I returned the boiled vegetables, which I had previously drained, and the salad were beautifully set out on the table, but there were no potatoes.

"Where are the potatoes?" I asked.

"I turned them off. You told me they were ready. They are in the pot on the cooker where you put them."

I thought she had drained them and was keeping them warm but, no, they were still in the water. After she had turned the electric ring off they must have continued boiling for a while. By the time I looked at them they were completely mushy. I looked at her questioningly. She looked back.

"What is wrong?"

"The potatoes are still in the water?"

"I know."

I realised that she had not been exaggerating. She could not cook anything.

The next day she said, "Today I want to cook the potatoes - just tell me for how long."

"It depends on the size. This size say eighteen minutes. They keep boiling on mark 2."

After eighteen minutes the buzzer rang. Then came Elizabeth's voice, "Tadek, Tadek, come here. I think the potatoes are still hard."

I looked; the potatoes were not even boiling. She had switched the ring to mark 2, enough to keep them boiling but not to start cold water boiling. I had forgotten to tell her it took eighteen minutes from the moment they started boiling.

Life was going to be fun! Elizabeth was the best girl in the world. I bought some cookery books and a pair of scales. We were going to have some guests and she was going to prepare the main course.

"It says two ounces. How many grams is this? There are two scales here, with grams on one, and ounces and pounds on the other. How do you work it all out?"

I explained.

When it said half an ounce, she would weigh out precisely half an ounce, not a pinch more or less. When it said stir gently, she would ask what gently meant. The dish was delicious.

I suggested I would prepare the first course and asked her what she would like to have.

"Melon and rum."

"Melon and rum? Very well. I shall go out and buy some rum." We have a well-stocked bar, but rum we rarely drink.

When I returned she asked, "Is it thinly sliced?"

I was puzzled. I probably misunderstood.

"I do not know much about rum. I just asked for a bottle."

"A bottle?" she asked as puzzled as I was when she asked whether it was thinly sliced.

Whilst she worked in the kitchen I put the melon onto appropriate plates and poured a bit of rum on it. Melon and brandy I had heard of, but not melon and rum. Elizabeth was Brazilian. Perhaps it was a common dish in Brazil.

Then I brought a plate with a slice of melon and some rum on it and asked, "Enough rum, or shall I pour some more on?"

"What is this? I asked for rum, rum, you know ramon! Prosciutto!"

It dawned on me. The Brazilians pronounce the "R" and the "H" in a way which at that time sounded identical to me. She meant melon and ham.

"But I told you I bought a bottle," I said.

"Well, I thought perhaps you buy sliced 'rum' in bottles or tins in the first world," she answered.

The guests were about to arrive. They were good friends and ate the melon and rum.

Elizabeth was a highly educated woman. She had travelled round the whole of Europe, and North and South America. She had studied for some time at Cambridge. However, I knew there would be misunderstandings. Life would be fun.

She did come from the third world, technologically advanced, but so different. A large proportion of women cannot cook. Everybody who is anybody has a servant or two and may have a driver. In my parents-in-law's house there was no shoe polish. Somebody on the corner will polish them for you; you drive there. Why the maid cannot do it, I do not understand. When the cook or maid-cook has her day off you go to a restaurant. The quantity of food on the table is at least twice as much as can possibly be eaten. "Everybody" in São Paulo has a house or flat in town and another one on the beach. Though you usually only go to the latter at weekends, a maid will be there as well. Self-service petrol stations were tried but did not work. Nobody is prepared to get out of the car into heat. In addition to the servants, however many there may be, someone will come once a week to clean the walls, floors, carpets, chandeliers, etc. It is a different world, but a rapidly changing one.

We tried to lead a "normal" life. I was a reasonably good cook. Elizabeth prepared beautiful salads and set the table to perfection. Since I cooked I was not allowed to do any washing up. In Brazil the maid did everything. In England she was the maid and I the butler. It worked. She always smiled. The house began to become a restaurant and boarding house. Guests came from all over the world.

Both my sons were living with their girlfriends by then, the girls they were later to marry. Aleksander's partner, Denise, was a charming girl; I had liked her from the day he had brought her to my house to introduce her. Cathy, Marius's partner, I knew less well; she was more difficult to get to know, but I felt that there was something "spiritual" about her. I liked her just as much. I still feel that she has something very "intuitive" about her, and that there will come a time when it will suddenly burst out and become obvious to everybody. Both sons seemed to be happy.

I was worried if they would take to Elizabeth or feel that their father was deserting them. When I told Marius what I felt for Elizabeth his answer was simple.

"Why don't you marry her, Dad?"

Elizabeth liked them both. There would be no problems there. She wanted me to invite them and their partners regularly, once a week or once a fortnight.

"Invite your ex-wife as well. You will always remain a family. She is the mother of your sons. Family life is very important."

"I would love to. I shall try. Your customs in Brazil are similar to the ones I was brought up with by my parents. In England they are different. Children like to feel independent of their parents. Most divorced couples feel that the other side was at fault and do not want to have anything to do with their ex-partners. The deep spiritual connection which is so prevalent in Brazil and in Poland, where I was born, is not so natural in England. I would love our family to remain a unity."

"Your mother, she is a very sick woman. Do you not think it would be better if she lived in your house? You could look after her better."

"I suggested it to her but she was afraid that being in my house she would spoil my chances to find a partner. The prospective partner would be afraid that she, my mother, would be the lady of the house."

"Hm."

The next time we went to my mother, Elizabeth told her that it would be better for her and me if she lived in my house. Yet when I suggested to Elizabeth that we should consider getting married her answer was simple.

"Why? If we love each other we can be together. We do not have to marry."

There was some fear in her. She had managed her own life for thirty-six years. She had been waiting for me but she did not know it. She had

had many boyfriends, but had refused all proposals. Then I did not understand the fear or uncertainty. Now I think I do. I recognised her as the one I was waiting for only two years and again nine years after we had met. She did not recognise me at those times, just as I did not recognise her the first time I saw her.

Elizabeth returned to Brazil. Two months later I flew to São Paulo. There was no longer any doubt that we would remain together - not in my mind and I think not in hers or her parents' or indeed my mother's.

My interest in the esoteric field increased rapidly. When I arrived in Brazil I started asking where one could find "psychic surgeons" - people who could open the body by running a finger or blunt object along it. Then, so I had heard, they could remove things from the body, all with or very little blood spilling. I had seen videos of such operations taken by a friend when he was in the Philippines. Since I knew him, I believed these films to be genuine. In one case some doctors from Germany and Switzerland had placed a mildly radioactive solution in a container into a body opened by psychic surgery. Then a Geiger counter showed that the patient was carrying the solution. The next day the psychic surgeon removed it.

I asked the then chairman or vice-chairman, I do not remember which, of the São Paulo Spirita Medical Association whether he knew of any psychic surgeon. He was an orthodox lung specialist, a consultant at the Oswaldo Cruz Hospital and a charming middle-aged man who spoke good English.

"Do you believe psychic operations are possible?"

"I don't know. I want to find out."

"Think," he said. "It takes a doctor five years of university study, then years of hospital practice to do what some say the simple unqualified people can do. Of course it is impossible."

We had a long chat. He believed as any spirita must, otherwise he would not be a spirita, that one could cure some seemingly incurable diseases by the "laying on of hands" and concentration on the patient - but an operation, no, that was impossible.

It was an attitude difficult to understand. The spirita, at least twenty per cent of Brazil's population even if they do not officially belong to any spirita organisation, believe that disincarnated spirits can incarnate temporarily into a human body, and speak as well as perform various other feats using this body. To me it seemed that if one chooses to believe that a spirit can cause brain impulses which make a person say things which are not stored in his brain, then one has to accept that the same spirit can cause movements of the hands which perform an operation. No university study is required. Only the spirit needs to have the relevant knowledge. I did not argue. It showed me again that some people have a blockage which makes it impossible for them to accept certain events.

The same doctor spoke in the following year about psychic operations as though he had always accepted them and was quite prepared to help me conduct scientific experiments to prove that they are a reality. The block had gone.

Elsie Dubugras, the editor of *Planeta*, on the other hand told me that of course psychic surgeons existed. Many who pretended to be one were fakes while others were real. She knew of none at the time in or near São Paulo who would physically open the body, but she knew one who performed "operations" without opening the body and was quite prepared to drive down with us to Sorocaba, some sixty miles from São Paulo, to see Geraldo de Padua, a chemical technologist, who was also a psychic surgeon.

We talked to Geraldo before he started his healing session. He explained that it is not he who works on patients, but one of two spirits each specialising in different types of ailments. During the healing sessions, his own spirit would probably leave his body. Sometimes it watches the proceedings. He was completely sincere. He does not charge, nor does he accept gifts. If people insist on showing their gratitude for being healed he gives them a list of charities they can donate their money to.

His father built for him a healing centre somewhat resembling a chapel. He is a "Christian" but does not belong to any one sect and believes that all religions are equally good if practised sincerely. Although some of the ceremonies preceding the healing resemble those of the Kardec Spiritists, he calls himself a "Universitalista".

On both sides of the healing area stand a number of mediums who also incorporate other spirits during the healing session. There are usually some one hundred people there but only fifty will be treated by him. Some come to receive general healing or to accompany their friends. Each "patient" is given a number when he arrives. When the healing starts the patient tells an assistant or Geraldo, or rather the spirit who at this time inhabits Geraldo's body, what his problem is. He will then be helped to lie down on an "operating" table and Geraldo will do one of many things.

He may pass a blunt object over a part of the body which needs investigation. The patient has the feeling that the flesh is parted. He will then concentrate, press here and there and then pronounce that he has done what is necessary to cause a cure. He may ask the patient to come back for more treatment. He may prescribe a medicine which is usually an orthodox or herbal substance. He may, as he did in my case the first time I saw him, say, "Everything is as well as it can be. It is all clean. You are all right." The reason I gave him, or the spirit working through him, for wanting my body looked at was that my hip, which had been broken in several places, sometimes caused me pain and became arthritic, even though I had learned by then how to remove the arthritic symptoms to such an extent that they did not show on X-rays for many months after I concentrated on them. I thought he might rebuild my hip so that it would be as it had been before the accident. I had heard of this being done. Similar miracles occur at Lourdes and other healing places. Those who are interested can verify this quite easily.

Most healers are deeply religious, not necessarily Catholic or even Christian. They believe in God. I did not know then that there is a good reason why "miracles" are performed on some and not on others. Some need the pain and inconvenience of an illness to do what they are meant to do or to remind them that their body is fragile; some need pain in order to learn something. For some a limited period of pain and inconvenience is all they need.

Geraldo and the spirits working through him were quite happy to talk and explain matters to Elizabeth and myself.

"Why the use of a blunt object pretending to cut routinely?"

"Most people need this to believe that something is being done. A cooperation between the healing energy and the person to be healed is helpful, particularly if the cure is to be of a permanent nature. In the past, and some energies still do it, the flesh was really cut and obstructing parts removed. This made the patient feel better. The energies working through me no longer do it. It is not necessary now. They dematerialise and heal using energy. If I think the patient badly needs material proof, I can cause a scar to appear where the operation was done."

Indeed this occasionally happened.

Sometimes Geraldo poured some water from a bottle into a glass, water on which he had previously concentrated, then held the glass near the patient's sick part of the body, organ, bone or whatever it was, removed the glass and pronounced the cure to have been effected. Sometimes he said, "No", concentrated on the water again, and once more held it near the affected part of the body.

During the whole healing session I was taking photographs of the healing as well as the mediums standing around and the patients waiting. After I had the photographs developed, several interesting phenomena appeared. One concerned the "water in the glass" healing. During one cure I had taken a photograph (a) before Geraldo concentrated on the water, (b) after he concentrated on it, (c) after he had placed it near the sick part of the body, (d) after he concentrated again on it because it had not done its job and (e) after he had placed it again near the sick part of the body. At first (a), it appeared transparent, after concentrating on it (b), it appeared milky, after being held near the sick part of the body (c), it was transparent again, after concentrating on it again (d), it was again milky, and finally after being placed again near the sick body (e), it was again transparent. This happened in another sequence when the cure was effected with the first glass of water. I did not notice this effect when I first looked at the photographs; Elizabeth did as she is more perceptive. But neither of us had noticed anything happening to the water with our eyes when watching the "psychic operations". I can only explain this by assuming that some energy was introduced into the water which our eyes could not perceive, but whose nature was such that it did cloud the film. Simple X-rays would have done the same. They too would have been invisible to the eye but would have appeared on the film. When the glass of water was held near the body this energy went from the water into the body, and the water appeared clear again.

There were other effects in the photographs which our eyes had not seen, such as colourful bands or a colour being superimposed on a normal background. When I showed these photographs to Elsie Dubugras, the editor who had introduced us to Geraldo, she was not surprised. She showed me photographs with similar anomalies which others had taken. This was not the only time I was to find the peculiar "effects" on photographs.

This is nothing compared with the photographs collected by a member of the Society for Psychical Research in London. They showed not only similar effects to those I had obtained but also "ghosts" in the shape of human beings, sometimes of deceased relatives of those taking the photographs or of people in the photographs. These ghosts might have their feet under the table and the rest over, or appear to be crossing a road but having no legs, etc. None were seen by those who were taking the photographs.

During this first healing session given by Geraldo which we experienced we saw grateful patients bring X-rays confirming "miraculous" cures and heard others speak of inexplicable cures. The Dutch television filmed a case of a partially paralysed man being cured by the entity acting through Geraldo; a member of a Japanese TV team which came to film Geraldo at work was healed of polio, if I remember correctly. We were told of people being cured of cancer and other "incurable" diseases. But certainly not everybody is cured.

After Geraldo has done his work, one or two of the mediums working with him will concentrate on the patient to bring him back into full equilibrium. He is then expected not to eat any meat until the next day.

We have since then seen Geraldo and observed him in action many times. The energies working through him call me "the man who takes pictures". Geraldo told us he will permit any investigation. He is prepared to have electrodes put onto his head provided people respect what is being done. The energies at work in these cases are subtle. Intense disbelief, scepticism or antagonism will usually neutralise or disturb them.

Some seem incapable of believing what they see and will insist that it is all "tricks" and that conjurors can do the same. Maybe. If they can heal, then they are also healers. When sceptics see photographs of an unusual nature they will say that they are "trick photographs". Since I have taken some of them, I know they are not. I used to try and prove that they were real, but have learned that it is pointless. If people are not ready to believe they will not do so. Sometimes even if they have accepted the reality of the impossible because the evidence was overwhelming, a few weeks later they will deny that they have ever accepted it. "If it is not reproducible, it is not scientific."

We met Hernani Guimaraes Andrade, chairman of the Brazilian Institute of Psycho-Biophysical Research, a charming retired engineer who is particularly interested in reincarnation and has published several papers and books on "spiritual" phenomena. During one of our visits to him we met Raul Correa Filho, at that time head of the physical chemistry department of the Brazilian Aerospace Institute (CTA) and a professor. Raul, who has become a personal friend of ours, is an interesting person. He is first a scientist and some of his work is devoted to proving scientifically the existence of another "dimension". Only if it can be proved scientifically will scientists and most people accept it, is his opinion. I too used to think this to be very important. I no longer do. I now feel that when a person is ready for it he will accept it whether it is "scientifically" reproducible or not. But I accept that if he can devise experiments to prove the existence of another "dimension" or "other forces", it will help many to accept aspects of the "spiritual" field. This would be good.

The interesting aspect of Raul is that he "sees" spirits. They are shadowy beings superimposed on the "solid" surroundings.

Once when we invited him to have lunch with us he described a "spirit", probably one of my "guides", who was somewhere behind my left shoulder. The interesting point about this was that his description was very close to that made by a simple young woman two years earlier, when I knew little or nothing about "spirits". She was a friend of a friend who happened to arrive whilst I was there. I was told she was rapidly developing into a medium so I asked her to say something about me. She told me much I knew to be true and also that I was somehow connected to many parts of the world. There were "threads" going from me to various areas of the globe. I asked her rather bluntly if she was telepathic since I was thinking at that time of a Planet Network.

"No," she said. "Well, perhaps sometimes. Right now there is a man behind your left shoulder in a white flowing robe, probably an Arab, telling me all I am telling you."

The "spirit" that Raul described was also in a white flowing robe.

CHAPTER 8

God's Favourite Children
It is now time for them to mature: when the student is ready the teacher appears.

"Take off the long-sleeved shirt and your tie - it is going to be a scorching hot day," Elizabeth said.

"Maybe, but it is the 23rd of December, your father's birthday. I cannot appear without a tie." I was still very formal and had not acquired the Brazilian informality.

The day was hot, about 35° C and no wind. I did perspire and had to change my shirt, but I retained my tie. So did Elizabeth's father. He is one of the very few Brazilians I know who nearly always wears one. After lunch "a few" relatives and friends came. I lost count; there must have been over fifty people. The Christmas tree was already decorated. It was a peculiar feeling to be in mid summer and yet know that the next day was Christmas Eve.

It was 24th December 1988. I brought several tapes of Polish, English and German Christmas carols and had them playing all day whilst Elizabeth and I were putting the final touches to the decorations. I had brought twenty teddy bears dressed as Father Christmas from England - one for each "child" and one for Elizabeth's father who was a child at heart.

Christmas dinner in Brazil is on Christmas Eve at about 8.00 pm. Traditional Christmas food includes imported traditional Central European delicacies such as dried fruits and nuts. Turkey and baked ham also feature prominently and there is a mid-European family atmosphere. The festivities take place in the grandparents' home and the whole family arrives. Grandchildren all run around excitedly, sometimes spotting Father Christmas on a sleigh coming down from the stars.

"I can see him!"

Perhaps it was a falling star, perhaps imagination or perhaps really Father Christmas? All windows are open to get a little movement of air and give the children a chance to spot Father Christmas on his sleigh.

The children are too excited to sit long at the dinner table. On the various TV channels, there are Christmas stories, some featuring Father Christmas coming through the snow. Most children have never seen snow. It does not exist in Brazil, not even in the mountains. They watch the snow scenes with wide-open eyes. So do I as I love snow at Christmas.

As midnight approaches, the excitement grows. Suddenly a knock is heard and a shout goes up, "Papai Noel." They run to the front door, open it, but nobody is there; then another knock and this time at the back door, but again nobody is there; finally a knock on the front door again and this time Father Christmas is there, complete with red boots, white snow cloak, enormous white beard and, dragging behind him, a big white sack. How he managed to survive I do not know. Difficult enough when the indoor temperature is 22° C, but when it is over 30° C he must be melting under the beard. He opens the sack and one of the adults takes out of it a smaller sack and shouts out a name. One of the children shouts, "I, I," and receives the smaller sack - full of goodies, an English teddy bear dressed as Father Christmas, some English crayons I had brought (foreign things are always more fun), a small drawing pad with English writing on it and a number of other little things which Elizabeth had thought of. Many suspect that Elizabeth helped Father Christmas in his choice. No wonder she is the favourite aunt. Though she has no children of her own, she has a dozen or two who love her. Christmas without her is not Christmas, many have told me. There is something very special about her, which is impossible to explain. People group round her and ask her for advice. If she stops in the road or at an airport somewhere, anywhere in the world, even if she does not speak the language of the country, people will ask her where a theatre, street, the lake or a concert is. It is as though she had "Information" written on her forehead.

Every time she came to England or left it, she had at least 50 kg of luggage, once over 70 kg. The flight allowance is 20 kg; whilst others had to pay for the excess weight she never did. When friends fly somewhere with a large excess, she takes them to the check-in, smiles, does all the talking and they never have to pay. Sometimes it is quite uncanny. When she wants something to happen it nearly always does, no matter what country she is in, Europe, America, Third World or Middle East. She is not the only one; there are other people who have things going their way without trying. In the past I did not understand why. I am not sure that I do now, but I feel that one factor is an energy which each of us emanates. Some of these energies blend with nearly every other energy and form a harmonious whole. Those who have this gift are usually contented people, rich or poor, who are in harmony with their surroundings, even if they have, as in Elizabeth's case, a very marked physical defect, which would make others bitter.

The 25th of December. There are vast quantities of food left over from the Christmas Eve celebrations. The family comes again, all bleary-eyed, few of whom went to bed before 2.00 am. But the conversation is lively. Some friends also come. This is one of the few days when there are no maids so we do the washing up ourselves. On Christmas Eve we pooled our maids with those of some relatives, so the kitchen was clean. From this point of view receptions are much easier in the Third World, as Brazil likes to call itself. Until 1994 maids were paid about $60 per month; in 1995 their pay doubled; soon not "everybody" will be able to afford a maid.

"We shall have an early night," Elizabeth told me. "Prepare the things you want to take to the beach. Don't forget the white outfit for the New Year."

"What white outfit?"

"Don't you remember we bought you white trousers? You have got a white shirt. On New Year's Eve everybody dresses in white."

The maid has come back from her family.

"Do you want to come with us to the seaside?"

"Yes," with hesitation. Fear? "I have never seen the sea."

Many of them have come down from north-east Brazil where they lived in very poor conditions. Many do not know how to eat with a knife and fork, and have at first difficulties in eating food which is normal for us. Often they are illiterate and have to be taught to cook, serve and write enough to put down at least the name of the person who telephoned. Of course many of them have never seen the sea. Our seaside flat has a tiny servant's room and shower, as all flats in Brazil have.

"Tadek, let's help taking down the food."

"What food?"

"For Guaruja." That is the seaside resort where our flat is.

"Why?"

"Because you cannot get fresh things there and it's more expensive."

We take all the left-overs and enough fruit and vegetables to feed ten people for ten days. I know we cannot possibly eat it all in the six days we shall be there. And of course we do not. Some comes back again, particularly since Elizabeth's father loves buying fresh fruit, which he buys even in Guaruja every morning. Nearly everything is available there, just round the corner. Bringing everything from São Paulo has become a custom. Others do it too. Nothing will persuade them that it is not necessary, just as they are certain that all imported things are better than local produce. There are even shops selling "only imported" goods. "Importado" is synonymous with good. I found many of the local products to be superb.

To transport Elizabeth's parents, her cousin and maid, we have to take both Elizabeth's and her father's cars. I drive one of them. Elizabeth, a very considerate and good person, is a superb driver but her normal speed is 60 miles per hour, the maximum permitted in Brazil. That is fine, but she also drives at 60 mph through the crowded streets of São Paulo. I begged her to drive a little more slowly because I would not be able to follow her. She is a considerate girl; she drove at 50 mph through the town but she did also stop occasionally to give me a chance to catch up.

Girls in Brazil usually are given a "Going Out" party when they are fifteen. Elizabeth did not want one. She wanted a car instead. She got one. The police never stopped her - again her incredible "luck"? The first time they did, because she looked too young to drive, was a few months after she turned eighteen and had taken her driving test.

The drive down to Guaruja was some 50 miles along a crowded winding motorway through innumerable tunnels. São Paulo is built on a plateau about 3000 ft above sea level. During weekends and holidays everybody who is "anybody" drives down to the sea. Guaruja, an empty and sleepy though ultra-modern seaside resort, becomes a roaring town with well over a million inhabitants.

Elizabeth's youngest sister and her two daughters come down as well.

Chapter 8

We unload our ton of food and vast quantity of clothing and go to the beach whilst the maids under mother's supervision prepare lunch. The beach, nearly two hundred feet wide and more than three miles long, is extremely crowded. Windsurfers, jet skiers, the water pulling you in, planes, and a helicopter above watching and occasionally fishing out a drowning person - it is certainly not a relaxing affair. Elizabeth is a superb swimmer, better than I, but she will not go in above her belly. She is right. Nearly every day somebody is pulled in and drowns. It is not the best place to swim but people love it and when empty it is beautiful.

Her brother has a house there and many other relatives have flats. Since we always go to more or less the same spot on the beach there is soon a colony of sun umbrellas around us and a party is in full swing.

Not only mad dogs and Englishmen but Brazilians too stay out in the midday sun (Guaruja is in the tropics), walking along the beach and playing in the water. Only after 1.00 pm do people start leaving the beach. The temperature may have reached 40°C. After lunch there is the siesta. Some but not all rooms are air conditioned which is better than São Paulo where for some inexplicable reason no private house or flat has air conditioning, however luxurious they may be in all other respects. Even penthouses with their swimming pools are sweltering in the hot summer. All offices, cinemas, shops and hospitals on the other hand are fully air conditioned. In winter it can get cold in São Paulo; 10° C is normal and sometimes it can be right down to 4° C at night; yet nobody I know has any form of heating. Why? Some have beautiful fireplaces, but they are there just for decoration, as are the traffic lights which nobody pays any attention to.

The Brazilians are children but perhaps God's favourite children. I feel certain Brazil will become the world's most important country. It is now time for the children to grow up. For reasons I cannot logically explain I feel certain they are about to do so.

On New Year's Eve we all go to Elizabeth's older brother's new house, standing on a hillside at the edge of Guaruja overlooking the sea, just the family and some close friends, probably sixty people, all in white. Music, dancing and games. It is a large house with a swimming pool. Some rooms are empty. When I walked into one of them to have a moment's peace, I noticed a tall cousin of Elizabeth with the name and figure of a Germanic

Goddess, one of her sun-tanned bosoms tipping out of her white dress, gently supported by a distinctly male hand and her dress raised on one side by the other male hand, with a brown statuesque leg protruding. Hoping they had not noticed me I left the room.

At midnight the beach below us seemed to explode. A hundred thousand fireworks went into the air and this kept on for many minutes - a sight not easily forgotten.

Then Elizabeth drove me down the winding road to the beach. There were innumerable small circles drawn on the sand. In their middle, one or more people were sitting in silence, with a candle burning, a bottle of wine, some food and perhaps some flowers. Not for personal consumption: this was an offering to the spirits, to the Mother of God or just an offering. Some may have sat there meditating for two hours. They would have been left in peace until a quarter to midnight when half or more of the town would go down to the beach. There were long queues in front of what I was told were mediums. They would tell people how they should behave during the following year and what was in store for them. Some would stand in the water with their back to the sea and jump three times over a wave. It is a world full of superstitions, taken only half seriously by most, but extremely seriously by some. A few even specialise in this and are paid to put curses onto others and many inexplicable things do happen.

A friend of ours, Guy Playfair, wrote an excellent book about Brazil which shows the different attitude to life which the Brazilians have, as well as many spiritual aspects which are unique to Brazil. He called it *The Flying Cow*. He explains his choice of title by the following story. A hard-worked executive in England, returning home one evening after a particularly exhausting day, tells his wife, "You will never believe this. Whilst driving back along the motorway I saw a cow flying right across the road." The wife grows a little pale, pours her husband a glass full of sherry and says, "Relax, darling. I'll be back in a moment." She goes to the telephone, rings their doctor and says, "Please come immediately. I think my husband is having a nervous breakdown. He is seeing things." The same happens in Brazil, but here the wife of the tired businessman pours him a tumbler of whisky and asks excitedly, "What colour wings did the cow have?"

Chapter 8

Nothing is considered impossible in Brazil.

Early in 1989 I returned to England. Mother was getting weaker and after Elizabeth persuaded her, she agreed to move into our house. I arranged a room for her which I had used as my office. It had its own side entrance as well as being part of the house, its own ensuite bathroom and a tiny storage room which was easily converted into a minute kitchenette. She was thus completely independent, yet part of our household. I hired an au pair girl who could do all the shopping and cleaning for mother.

On 1st June 1989 Elizabeth, her parents and her brother with his wife came to London and on 3rd June 1989 we had our engagement party, again in the garden with the roses in full bloom. My sons and their girlfriends were there, as well as my mother; the people I loved most surrounded us. The sound of birds provided the background music.

The only days I can remember when I was equally happy were the times when my sons were born. Aleksander the older one came just before midnight on 26th June 1962. I remember banging my head on the wall because I was so happy when he finally arrived after thirty hours of expectation in hospital. The younger one Marius was quicker about it; he arrived just before noon on 7th January 1966 at home before the doctor came. I, with a leg in plaster, delivered him. I had left the front door open so that the doctor could come in whenever he arrived. When he did, Marius's head was appearing. He took one look at what I was doing, sat down in a chair and said, "Continue, you are doing fine." Later the midwife turned up. A nine-pound baby had arrived. I was the happiest person on earth.

"Painless birthgiving" was in vogue then. It relied on a semi-hypnotic technique. My wife and I sang a simple rhythmic song whilst I helped her to bang her hand on the pillow in rhythm to the tune. She had no time to concentrate on the pain. From what she told me the birth was not painless but much less painful. The technique worked best if the husband cooperated; those who used it were very pleased with it. It is a pity that it went out of fashion, and that many doctors said it was too dangerous and giving birth in cold impersonal hospital surroundings was safer. Now we know that this is not true, provided sensible precautions are taken at home. We also know that children born at home are usually more at peace with themselves provided the mother was not afraid of the impending birth.

Is this not further proof that children's memory goes further back than many orthodox doctors will have us believe? Would it not be a good idea to combine ancient tradition, common sense and modern scientific knowledge? Much is being done about it recently; natural rather than chemical relaxation is considered more beneficial in both sickness and the birthing process. Sometimes the two are combined for best results.

The 3rd of June 1989 was as perfect as most important days had been in our joint past and continued to be in our future. That we celebrated in the garden I remember well, but the details seem to be behind a veil. I am sure all the memories are somewhere in my subconscious but in the conscious there is just a feeling of absolute bliss, of something happening that I had been expecting for ever.

My future parents-in-law were beautiful people. My mother-in-law exuded goodness and was always smiling. One of those people one cannot help but love, plump but with a pretty face and extremely agile. My father-in-law was the spitting image of Kojak, the "detective". When he put on sun glasses nobody could tell the difference. In the street people stared at him. The right parents for my wife to have. They liked me. I knew everything would be perfect. Although I spoke no Portuguese and they no English, I knew they liked me and I certainly liked them, another example of telepathic understanding or energy exchange. I am certain that this form of understanding, a type of telepathic communication, will within a few years become a frequently used form of communication. Not all, but many more than now will have this ability.

I do not know why, but I mentioned to Montague Keen, a very good friend of mine who lived in Suffolk, that I was developing an interest in parapsychological phenomena. He said that he too had an interest in these phenomena, but right then found it difficult to accept most of the metaphysical phenomena reported as real. If they could be proven scientifically he would be prepared to accept them. He told me he was a member of the Society for Psychical Research. It was the oldest society investigating seriously such phenomena and was based in London. I might find it interesting to join them. They gave frequent lectures on these topics, published new developments and had an annual conference which would soon take place. I should contact them, become a member if I wished and go to the conference which would be held in Bournemouth.

Chapter 8

I joined the SPR and went to the conference with Montague. Elizabeth did not come with me. She thought I should go alone. Why? I did not argue. She often knows what is best. I accept it. Six years later I was told the reason why she sometimes "knows".

I found the conference fascinating. Some aspects were particularly interesting. A large proportion of its members were lecturers and professors. Some of them I had known when I was still an active member of the teaching establishment myself. They had never talked about their interests in parapsychological phenomena. They were, perhaps rightly, worried that if people knew of their involvement it might hinder their scientific career. A few members were sceptical but one in particular was extremely sceptical and would not accept any unusual phenomena as a possibility. She thoroughly enjoyed taking part in public discussions and television programmes in which she would, in my opinion, show a complete lack of deeper understanding, and try to demonstrate that all unusual phenomena were either "cheated" or foolish and that everything could be explained by currently known physical and medical theory. She and many sceptics have obviously not heard of or thought about Heisenberg's uncertainty principle which clearly shows that science must accept uncertainty. Heisenberg was one of the greatest physicists of the century. They probably have also not thought of the implications of the fact that science shows conclusively that light consists of particles but also shows conclusively that it is a wave and not particles. Science as we know it at present cannot explain everything. Most advanced scientists accept this when they reach their limits.

Many of the topics discussed were fascinating, such as detailed studies of poltergeist phenomena, materialisation, healing and so on. One of the ladies reading a paper was Barbara Ivanova, a Russian parapsychologist who had published many papers in western journals but was in London for the first time. I knew that Russians had no western currency and suggested that she could stay in our house for a week or two after the conference. She accepted with great pleasure, particularly after she heard that my fiancee was a Brazilian.

Barbara spoke fluent "Brazilian" (Portuguese as the Brazilians do). She told us that she learned, or rather remembered, "Brazilian" in a few months - remembered because in her previous incarnation she was a Brazilian mulatto. Her English was also good but that took much longer to learn. Czech, which is a Slavonic language and therefore similar to Russian, she never mastered. German she had learned from her parents who were of German Latvian origin. Brazilian Portuguese, a completely different language, she "learned" to perfection.

Being the first Russian parapsychologist who came here legally, and indeed a lady of great knowledge in her field with several publications and an impressive healing power, she was invited to give lectures all over London. Reporters called frequently and the BBC interviewed her.

She stayed three months with us. They were a very full three months; people constantly called; we drove Barbara to various lectures, answered questions about her when she was not available and met innumerable new people.

The day before she was to go to Scotland to deliver a lecture at Findhorn, a Brazilian telephoned. "Is it true that Barbara Ivanova is staying with you?"

"Yes," Elizabeth answered in Portuguese, realising from the caller's accent that he was Brazilian.

"Dr Hernani called me from Brazil and said that you would introduce us to her. I am Dr Ney Peres. We are here, a whole group of Brazilians, visiting the Mind, Body and Spirit Exhibition. Can we meet Barbara?"

"Of course, but you will have to come tomorrow for breakfast because she is leaving at noon for Scotland."

"Thank you; do not bother with breakfast. We shall eat early in our hotel and be with you at 9 o'clock. There are very many of us."

Most unusual for Brazilians they arrived on time, a dozen or so of them. They were all professional people - engineers, doctors and psychologists. Barbara was to them a fascinating phenomenon - a Russian who spoke fluent Brazilian and was in her previous incarnation herself Brazilian. Most Brazilians, no matter what their religion, accept reincarnation as a fact. Some very staunch Catholics only consider it a possibility, but even some priests accept it as a fact.

Whilst I was preparing coffee in the kitchen (our living-dining-kitchen area is semi-open plan) I heard a peculiar noise and then Elizabeth's raised voice.

"Come quickly. Eliane is receiving."

Receiving? Whom or what I wondered, but came immediately. There was a young lady who had been introduced as a clinical psychologist, her face twisted in a most unusual expression, sitting on the floor. I thought she was having an epileptic fit. Peculiar sounds emerged from her mouth - a word or two of what might have been Russian and then German.

"Get a tape recorder, quick," Elizabeth commanded.

Eliane started speaking fluent Spanish. Her face settled down to a fixed expression, no longer twitching. Then it changed expression and she spoke Portuguese. I held the tape recorder close to her. Ney was also taping her.

From time to time Elizabeth who was further away interrupted with a question. Everybody else was perfectly silent.

When Eliane's mouth stopped talking, her body and her face gave a slight twitch again and the expression changed to her normal self.

In the meantime, I had realised what had happened. It was my first experience of seeing an "outside spirit" enter, take charge of and leave again a human body, a body which had had little or no experience of such things happening to it. Later I was to see this frequently. Experienced mediums just give a slight jerk and frequently their facial expression changes slightly when they, as the Brazilians call it, "receive" a spirit. People to whom this had not happened before, or only rarely, and who did not know how to react, usually twisted their faces; sometimes their bodies seemed to go into a convulsion; sometimes they emitted a peculiar sound, quite frightening if one is not used to it. Their voice invariably changed slightly or completely. The spirit who took charge of their body, when asked who he was, might say that he was a spirit of someone who had died and had something to say to us "living" humans. Sometimes the answer was that the energy who took charge of the body was one that had never incarnated. Sometimes it was a "group" energy; sometimes these energies or spirits had something interesting and valuable to say; sometimes they seemed to be "lost" energies causing the medium to emit peculiar high-pitched sounds. Sometimes, I now believe, they are "lost" spirits, and just want to show that they exist.

During this and the following year Eliane, when she was still not very experienced, "received" all these types of energies. Mediums can be trained to reject energies which they do not wish to receive, to "protect" themselves from what some call evil energies.

What Eliane said, or the spirits that spoke through her the first time I witnessed this phenomenon, was intended for the Brazilians in the room. Perhaps it was also for me so that I would get an introduction to this field, and to plant the seed of "Atalanta".

Equally interesting was the fact that when I replayed the tape the voice which was speaking through Eliane was a whisper whilst Elizabeth's questions were loud and clear. On the tape of Ney, who stood a little further away, both Eliane's voice and Elizabeth's questions were equally loud. Later I was told that this was not an infrequent phenomenon. What was said was meant for Ney and his group of Brazilians, and not for me. What was even more perplexing was that when I tried to replay my tape a year later, some of Eliane's words and whole sentences were replaced by a completely different voice, distinctly male - that of Mathew Manning, a well-known English healer who also had other psychic powers.

A proof of Barbara Ivanova's healing powers was clearly demonstrated to me when I, whilst chopping some vegetables, also chopped the tip of my finger off. I tried to stick it on with some plaster and drive myself to a hospital, but using one hand to hold the part I chopped off, with blood everywhere, I could not get the plaster to stick. I called Barbara to help me.

She came and said, "Just let me try something. Perhaps you will not have to go to hospital."

"Whatever you want to do, do it quickly. I am beginning to feel very peculiar."

"Just hold the tip onto your finger where it ought to be."

She pointed the fingers of both her hands at my injury and within a minute the blood stopped flowing.

"Hold it a little longer."

Another two minutes passed.

"I think it will be all right if you let go."

I let go.

"Sit down now. No more blood will flow but don't wash your hand for half an hour."

I relaxed, switched on the radio with my good hand and began to feel perfectly normal again. Gently I washed my hands. The tip stayed on. By now there was not even a scar. The finger nail grew and the whole finger looks normal.

Barbara did not like healing. She preferred lecturing on esoteric topics, thought transfer and healing. She was, however, quite prepared to do demonstrations of healing. Once after talking about healing at a distance, we telephoned my wife's family in São Paulo and asked for various members who had health problems to come to the telephone. Barbara, after talking to them, managed to lower blood sugar and blood pressure, and cause the reduction of other problems which could be verified by medical tests.

Often when I asked her a question concerning metaphysical subjects, she would answer, "Ask me again during a lecture."

I later realised that somehow she would not know an answer when there were just one or two listeners present, but gave a lucid reply when she had a larger audience. Either she managed to tap into an energy source when she was surrounded by many people, since it potentiated her desire to be able to give an answer, or she drew energy from her audience, and the extra energy made it easier for her to tap into another energy source outside or perhaps within her, a source which had all the required answers. In spite of her deep knowledge of some aspects, I do not think that she ever considered more deeply that one person can potentiate the energy of another.

At the time she was in London I knew little about these matters, but later I found that most mediums do not realise or do not wish to realise that their knowledge could be more accurate and of more importance if they worked together and tried to potentiate each other's powers. Some even teach that this should be done, but do not do it themselves. They will even say that each has a different "package" to deliver. In recent years more mediums have at last begun to write that soon more of us, particularly if we work together, will be able to tap into a higher energy, joint energy or whatever term they may use. Indeed those who do so rather than rely on individual aspects of this energy or "spirits" seem to come up with a similar prognosis of the probable future. The sensible ones of course realise that no future prognosis can be certain since we have a free will. We are not machines which are programmed.

Before Christmas 1989 we went to Brazil again. I now knew a little more about the impossible but the "scientist" in me still wanted more incontrovertible proof. I wanted amongst other things to see with my own eyes people being cut open with a knife, bits of their body removed which I could take home, and the resulting wound closed by just pressing the flesh together and to be sure that no infections occurred later.

I was told of a person who without any medical training did this. Elizabeth and I asked whether we could attend such a psychic operation session and as always were given permission to do so. We asked Raul Correa, our scientific Brazilian friend, who, so he said, could see spirits, to come with us.

Operations of this nature are not permitted in Brazil. Mauricio, the gentleman we were about to observe performing them, operated in a different house every time he came to São Paulo. If anybody had even complained that he had been hurt Mauricio would of course face a court case, but as long as nothing went wrong the government pretended not to know where he was operating.

When we arrived there was a long line of prospective patients. Mauricio, as most Brazilian healers, does not charge; those who do lose their power or die, so most Brazilians believe. He was going to operate in a reception room in the back garden of a large expensive house. We had been introduced as serious investigators, and were conducted to the front of the room in which the operations were going to occur.

Just before Mauricio appeared Raul said he could perceive several "spirits" approaching. When Mauricio arrived, a full-set medium height man obviously from a simple background, he or at least his mouth asked us to come right in, observe everything from whatever position we wanted and take whatever photographs we wanted. When he started operating, often without looking where he was cutting, and frequently talking to us at the same time, Raul said that one spirit was responsible for the movement of one of Mauricio's hands, another for the other hand and a third one for what Mauricio was saying to us. He cut away merrily with extreme speed. An "operation" lasted at the most three minutes. Whilst cutting he often looked at us, though his eyes had a vague expression. I asked him why he said that Dr Fritz was operating through him. A number of psychic surgeons in Brazil claim that Dr Fritz is operating through them. No well-known surgeon by that name is known to have existed. "He" explained that Dr Fritz is the name a group of spirits have given themselves.

Some people who came to him suffered from Aids. He took blood out of a vein in their arm with a syringe and injected it into their stomach. I was told that he has healed many.

Perhaps the most impressive operations were on the eye. He cut the skin of the surface of people's eyes with a pair of rounded nail scissors. After an operation was completed in two minutes or so the patient got up from the "operating" table, put a cloth on his eye, sat on a chair for five minutes, took the cloth away, got up and said he could see much better.

Raul left well before Mauricio finished; he had been operating from about 9.00 pm to 2.00 am.

When he was "himself" again, I asked him whether he knew how he "operated".

"Yes, " he said. "One spirit takes control of my right hand, another of my left and a third speaks, tells the patient what to do and today spoke to you."

This was exactly what Raul told us was happening. To what extent Raul "sees" the spirit and to what extent he "senses" them is still not quite clear to me. What is the difference between "seeing" and "sensing"? Both make us aware of the existence of some non-physical entity. Do we "see" or "sense" objects and people in our dreams?

Mauricio also explained that although one object of the "spirits" was to help people, another was to show in an incontrovertible manner that they exist and that they can help us, and co-operation between incorporated and non-incorporated spirits will lead to a more rapid development and elevation of humanity, and that this is in the spirits' interest. When they become incorporated they will learn more; much of the learning can only be done while incorporated, i.e. being permanently in a body. Only after they have learned enough can they move to a higher level.

"You and Elizabeth are important. You are a scientist. People will believe you. Ask anything you like."

An increasing number do believe us now, but not all. Elizabeth and I have found that physical proof will not convince those who do not want to believe. They will say it is all "conjuring tricks". They are simply not able to accept the "impossible". Under Elizabeth's guidance I have learned to understand that people will believe only as much as they are ready to believe.

Give them a chance to read about or witness unusual phenomena and the existence of "other forces", but do not insist. It will only make them unhappy and confused if you do and in the end they will reject it, giving any reason they can think of. This will continue until they are ready to accept it, which may not be in this life. Nevertheless, it is good to give people a chance to see the truth.

I began to have a dilemma: is one really allowed to heal using "spiritual "phenomena? Is one not interfering in God's domain? It took me months to accept an answer to this question. Of course one can use any method available when healing, such as chemistry and the knife, and also spiritual techniques. They are all gifts which God gave us. What we are given we should use, otherwise it is wasted. If anything is a sin, wasting a gift certainly is. But even having realised all this, I still feel uncomfortable with the idea of organ transplants. Somewhere in the background I feel that if a vital organ gives up, perhaps one ought to die. Of course this is completely irrational; I might as well say that if one has pneumonia one should not use antibiotics as the person is meant to die; or if I feel that one should not be kept alive by means of somebody else's organ, I should reject blood transfusion. Yet it never occurs to me that there is anything wrong with transfusion. All or at least many of us, including myself, have irrational aspects to our "character".

I brought back to London bits of body cut out by "spiritual energy" which I had pickled in alcohol. It was no proof of anything to those who did not want to accept it. I could have got them from an orthodox operating theatre.

It is probably also true that some of the "psychic surgery" is charlatanism, conjuring or other forms of cheating. To the best of my knowledge I have not come across any, but I have observed in action only those who do not charge for their work.

After our return to London early in 1990 Rosemary Steel telephoned.

"I know you started to take an interest in the scientifically inexplicable. In the real meaning of life. Can you help as co-organiser?"

I had met Rosemary for the second time in my life last year when she was looking for Barbara Ivanova, the Russian parapsychologist, and somebody had given her my telephone number but not my name. When she heard me answer she said immediately, "I know you. You are the scientist who was interested in Kirlian photography."

Indeed I had met her a few years ago when I first started taking an interest in energy emanations from human bodies and, as I found, all living bodies. I had attended a brief workshop which she gave. She is probably the most knowledgeable person in the psychological interpretation of Kirlian photography in England. What she told me about myself was certainly very true - an able but tense person, not permitting his real self to emerge, whose life could change dramatically if he was prepared to alter some small aspects of his mode of living, perhaps his interests. She went into some detail which I thought was pertinent. I made a mental note to look into it more deeply. I did not; I was obviously not ready.

Rosemary was going to organise the second world congress of Kirlian photography. She had told me so last year and we had found one or two people who would help and a Brazilian who would come and give a lecture and workshop. Now she wanted me to be co-organiser. Good - I was ready for it. I knew that organising events, and later much more, which lay on the borderline of the orthodox and unorthodox, and in particular events which formed bridges between the two, was going to be not only my but also Elizabeth's work for the next few years.

Rosemary's telephone call searching for Barbara and finding me was not a coincidence. It was synchronicity, something that happens with increasing frequency to many people. Though at the time I had hardly heard of the term, I was noticing that when I wanted to meet somebody, experience something or when someone wanted to meet me, it just happened, usually at the right time; rarely or never did I in recent times feel, "I wish it had happened before."

During the congress to which we had invited the most prominent workers in this field from literally every continent, I found that many orthodox medical practitioners were using the technique to help diagnose illness. I learned that some hospitals had cooperated and compared the diagnosis obtained from Kirlian photography with that obtained by conventional methods. There was obviously some radiation emanating from people which though invisible to the human eye could be captured on film. Yet because nobody can measure the radiation directly by instruments, most doctors reject it and are not prepared to experiment with it.

I also heard that because different methods for obtaining these "aura" photographs are used, they are not all identical. This gives those who find it difficult to accept facts which are not "scientifically" proven a good excuse for not accepting the validity or indeed medical use of them. It is also true that some techniques merely produce corona effects which have little to do with the patient's state of health.

Yet when proper techniques are used illness can often be diagnosed in early stages when orthodox medical tests would not indicate it. Furthermore, the "aura" photographs can indicate whether an illness or incipient illness is due to purely organic reasons or psychological reasons.

Kirlian or "aura" photographs do not heal a person but they can indicate the organ which is malfunctioning and causing whatever the symptoms are which the patient is complaining of. They can also be used to interpret the psychological make-up of a person. Often a combination of the two can explain symptoms which are otherwise difficult to interpret. Once the cause is understood, healing can be caused by orthodox or complementary medicine, or sometimes just by counselling which will modify the attitudes of patients.

I also met people there who could see the aura with the naked eye. Is this the reason why so many pictures of saints show them to have a halo around their head? Could some painters, who are often sensitive people, see these auras? Though Kirlian photographs usually use hands and feet because technically this is easiest, those who see auras with their naked eye see them around the whole body, particularly the head. This is where Kirlian, a Russian X-ray technologist, photographed them accidentally. Later he tried to explain where these "aura" effects appearing on the photograph had come from.

Although some doctors use Kirlian photographs to get an initial indication of the cause of the symptom which the patient complains of, the method is not widely used by orthodox practitioners.

Acupuncture, now generally acknowledged and used, was also not an "acceptable" form of treatment in the West until recently, although it has been in use in China for millennia and is part of the medical course there in orthodox colleges, where it is often used for anaesthetising purposes. A doctor inserts and twists one or two needles positioned in strategic places in the patient's body, whilst one or more other doctors perform an operation without any chemical anaesthetics. Some such operations were performed in the West and shown on television. Slowly acupuncture has become an accepted tool.

In a few years Kirlian photography may become an equally accepted diagnostic tool.

As a result of my interest in psychic phenomena I was advised to meet Dr Nubor Facure, head of the Brain Institute of the University of Campinas, one of Brazil's foremost universities. He is, in addition to being an orthodox doctor, a practising Kardec Spiritualist and sometimes combines the knowledge of the psychic with the orthodox when treating his patients.

He invited me to give a lecture to a group consisting mainly of doctors and other University staff. I chose as a title "Brazil, the centre of spiritual development". My wife quite rightly reacted by saying that I knew next to nothing about Spiritualism and particularly the Brazilian brand. But the title came to me instantly when asked to deliver the lecture, and I was beginning to learn to trust my intuition.

The next day I sat down to make some notes on what I was going to say. Somehow "things" came to me. I was confident that I could speak for an hour and get off my chest some matters about which I felt strongly. I spoke no Portuguese so Elizabeth was going to translate. She hated being in the limelight and in particular in front of TV cameras. But whenever I spoke in Brazil she sat next to me and translated.

What I said included some of the following: I had felt for some time that from an economic point of view Brazil should lead the world. Now I felt that it should also do so from a spiritual point of view. Perhaps "lead" is the wrong word; inspire, though still not quite right, is better. I felt something developing in Brazil; although the Brazilians are children they have something in them that is attractive and will soon blossom. They are still children and I felt at that time, as I do now, that there is a fight going on inside them; they would like to shine and do what is right, and yet are afraid to do so. I read Alice Bailey's statement that "Brazil has the seed but does not know it" much later, but I felt it instinctively then.

There is a higher percentage of people in Brazil than in any industrial country I know who seem to have some connection with levels which many of us do not quite understand, but if we contact them we receive abilities which are not explicable by current physical knowledge. They are abilities which some of us connect with a "spiritual" state. Much of it is good. It permits people to heal, to write about matters of which they have no conscious knowledge, and to see aspects of the probable future.

However, some of those who have an ability to use their unorthodox powers use them for, as far as immediate results are concerned, evil purposes. They cause people to become ill, to suffer and, so some say, to die, although I have not witnessed it. Some believe that these evil forces try to prevent the positive forces from doing their work, because they realise that too much high-level work will be done in Brazil. People at all levels from a simple street-cleaner to a university professor accept this.

Is there really a struggle between good and bad, and one has to win? I do not believe so; I feel it is simply an interplay between various energies, all of which are necessary for our development. There are less and more developed energies. Can a child who has little or no experience of what some of his actions can cause be said to be bad because one of these has caused what most would call a "tragedy"? Is the death of a person, however painful to those who love that person, really a bad occurrence? Could the death not have caused many people to lead a "better" life or made them to think deeper thoughts which would elevate their life?

Brazil is a rapidly maturing country. Many of the "evils" that happen could be there to cause a more rapid and ultimately higher elevation. What is necessary is the correct use of the free will and the desire to do what is good for the majority. The realisation that the general good will ultimately result in "personal" good is perhaps the most important development and is beginning to be voiced.

I said all this with a particular emphasis on the beautiful future I saw for Brazil and ended with the words, "I am sure I am right, particularly now when I am about to be officially married to the person I know I was always supposed to marry, the person without whom I would not know many of the things I now know, the person who is translating every word I am saying."

"The second day of spring," I continued, "the 22nd of September 1990, will be the official beginning of the second part of my life. Wish me the happiness which I know I shall experience and which I know you shall experience once the second part of your life starts. It will happen in the very near future."

Like so many Brazilians they knew what I said was true, yet did not want to believe it.

"The change will occur but not as soon as you see it. It is meant to happen but are we ready?"

They see the possibility and some the probability, but few at that time were prepared to use their free will to help make happen what they knew had to happen. So many were prepared to sit back and let happen what God and the "spirits" were going to cause to happen rather than work for it. Now five years later much is changing. More use their free will, perhaps the greatest gift humanity was given.

"We believe your divorce documents to be real, but our law demands that our embassy in London makes checks. It will take at least three months."

"Can you not telephone London? You could have a written answer in days."

"Possibly, but that is not the way we do it."

If something can be made difficult or complicated, the Brazilian authorities will find a way to do so. It seems to be something inherent in their way of doing things. They know it is wrong, yet refuse to do anything about it. Soon they will.

The Orthodox Cathedral in São Paulo is a beautiful church. When I first saw it two years earlier I said half jokingly, "We could get married here." Both Elizabeth and I are Roman Catholics by baptism, but we both believe there is one God who makes no distinction between Roman, Orthodox or any other Catholics, nor between members of any other religion.

When the authorities made difficulties with our civil wedding, I suggested we go to the Orthodox Cathedral and speak to the priests there. They were a delightful lot. If we loved each other they would do their best to help us get married. The fact that we were Roman Catholics and not Orthodox Catholics seemed to make no difference to them. They asked us to write an official request to the archbishop and promise that we would have a civil wedding as soon as we could, and arranged for our church wedding to take place in ten days on the 22nd September 1990. There was no time for official invitations, so Elizabeth phoned several friends. The word spread like wildfire. On the day the cathedral was full - not only Brazilians came and my best men were two Argentinians who arrived at the last moment.

The wedding was unrehearsed. Neither one of us had ever seen an Orthodox wedding. It is something much more complicated, but in my opinion more beautiful than a Roman Catholic one. The altar stands in the middle of a large platform. On one side stood Elizabeth and her eight witnesses and on the other mine, another eight, while I was in front of them.

At 3 o'clock the music started, the main door opened and Elizabeth, supported by her father, advanced slowly towards the altar accompanied by tunes by Tchaikovsky, whilst I came down equally slowly towards her. My feelings were those of pure joy, the fulfilment of a promise for which I had waited a lifetime. Others tell me that when the doors opened and Elizabeth appeared, a breeze of an unearthly energy went through the cathedral. I noticed tears appearing in many eyes. We met halfway, her father stepped aside and I led her the rest of the way to the altar.

It was a moment when I knew that more than logic, more than earthly love and more than fate had brought us together. An agreement on a different level had been made between us which could never be broken. I knew little about these matters then, but I knew that the contract we were about to sign was not one of this earth. It had nothing to do with what the church teaches and what is so frequently broken. It was something at a much deeper level.

The feeling of emotion, as described by others, was one of a quality which none had experienced before. It was as though two sounds had met which together produce an effect that defies description and can only be felt with one's whole being. Years later people still speak of it as something unique in their experience. Whatever the cause may have been, however at the time I tried to rationalise it, it was above physical description. It was as though an invisible veil had covered the whole congregation.

When we reached the altar the music changed to Paganini's theme which was used in the film *Somewhere in Time*. Often in time we had met before; somewhere in time we had been brought together to meet again

Chapter 8

and again. Two energies which are one as in due course all energy shall be one, was the thought that came to me.

I greeted Elizabeth's witnesses whilst she greeted mine. Then she greeted hers and I mine. I embraced each witness and kissed each lady's hand. Most of them had tears in their eyes. These were minutes of utmost beauty. During the service a crown made of flowers was placed on our heads and we walked three times round the altar, symbolising dancing round the altar which in turn was a symbol of the joy of earthly life. At least so it was explained to me. From time to time I took my wife in my arms and kissed her. Since I did not know the intricacies of the ceremony, I did what I felt was right or was indicated by gestures. Towards the end I kneeled and kissed my wife's hand. This was certainly not part of the normal ceremony. I felt I had to do it. The congregation felt they had to cry at this gesture.

As we walked out, nearly all the faces turned towards us had tears flowing down their cheeks and a smile on their lips. Even now when I look at the film of our wedding, my eyes become distinctly wet and some say that it has a healing quality.

We did not want a large reception; even so, more than a hundred guests turned up for the champagne, soft drinks and cakes. All large blocks of flats in São Paulo have the ground floor reserved for receptions and that is where we had ours.

During my speech I stated clearly and without any doubt that it was worth waiting over fifty years to find the best wife in the world and that I was the happiest man in the world. Maybe it was true at the time. I did not know that one could be even happier. Now I know that I was wrong. Five years later there is an even happier man in the world. It is the person I am now.

Elizabeth's younger brother-in-law Luiz gave us amongst other things a night in a luxury motel room. A motel in Brazil is something unique. It resembles other motels only in the fact that one drives into it in a car. The room is hired by the hour, not day. It may consist of a room with bath or a suite with sauna, swimming pool, jacuzzi, sliding roof, mirrors on walls and ceilings, round bed, flashing lights, TV and porn films, etc. Food, usually good, is ordered by telephone and served by being placed into a cupboard from the outside and the guest then opens the cupboard from inside the room and takes it out. He can eat it sitting in the jacuzzi or the pool, or eat it in bed or at a table.

The bathroom is invariably equipped with a toothbrush, shaver and condoms. There are lots of towels and sheets which can be put on the floor next to the jacuzzi, pool or on the carpet. Everything is there for making love in relaxed privacy and in any manner one's fantasy might create.

Motels are found everywhere: in towns, on motorways and along country roads.

This time all we used was the jacuzzi and the round bed, and even that not in the way it was meant to be used. The day had been too beautiful and too crowded; we just enjoyed the memories and the nearness of each other. We pressed a button to slide open the roof, enjoyed the stars above us for a while and then closed it again. We were the happiest couple imaginable, although we were fast asleep.

The next day we went to Elizabeth's Guaruja flat at the seaside together with my two "best men", Elizabeth's Argentinian friends. It was an unusual honeymoon, but we had had many honeymoons before and our bliss was different to that which a flight to say the Caribbean could provide. That I was not quite on this earth showed clearly in the evening when the four of us went to a restaurant. I complained that the lettuce was exceptionally tough. Horacio, one of the two best men, pointed out that I was trying to eat my napkin!

After our return to London we found my mother had been well looked after by our last au pair, a charming theatrologist called Teresa who spent half the day in school and the other half looking after mother. Though now married, she is still our friend.

Mother was overjoyed by our return, and even more that I was truly happy. I knew she would not live much longer. All she wanted from life on earth was to see her son settled with a wife of whom he was certain that she was the one he would share the rest of his life with. Somehow she knew that whoever he chose, now it would be the right choice. She knew that I had learned my lesson.

On 31st October we had our civil wedding in London. Mother, though weak and often short of breath, was serenely happy. She could not go unaided even the fifty feet into the garden, but was always smiling even when in pain. She was an inspiration to all who visited her.

Chapter 8

The 22nd of November was a warm day. It was her name day and we celebrated some of it in the garden. A day or two later she invited my sons and distributed between them all her remaining jewellery and the few gold sovereigns which she had saved for emergencies. Her voice was weak and she tired easily, so I explained the history of each piece.

She believed in a life after this life and I had to promise her not to hold her spirit down by modern medical techniques. On 2nd of December we started telephoning her friends and relations to say farewell. She whispered to me and I repeated it in a louder voice, explaining that she was perfectly happy and ready to go.

Some could not understand how I could say such things in her presence. They obviously found it difficult to share our feeling that death is but a form of graduation. One hopefully learns during this life all that one is meant to learn and then goes on to the next stage. There should be no regrets; some are meant to learn one thing and some another. All that matters is that one used one's greatest gift, the free will, correctly. Only the person whose will it is, knows whether he or she used it as it was supposed to be used.

We rang her two oldest friends, whom she had known from her school days, last, on 9th December 1990. Neither number answered. By then someone was sitting by her bedside all the time. At night it was invariably Teresa whom she liked deeply and who had helped to look after her during the last few months, or Zbyszek, the husband of an ex au pair of mine who happened to be visiting us at the time. They had a bell which they were supposed to ring if they thought mother's physical end was near.

CHAPTER 9

Graduation: Death is a Step to Another Level
*Our bodies are transient -
our spirits continue for much longer.*

In the early evening of 9th December we were still whispering with mother about some of the beautiful moments of her life. Then she fell asleep. Suddenly I knew. I called Elizabeth who was next door and whilst we prayed she took her last few breaths.

Although I have tears in my eyes as I write about this moment, I also remember it to be one of the most beautiful moments of my life. Elizabeth and I knew that her spirit was happy and going straight to where it was meant to go.

Three days later we found that one of the friends mother tried to ring on her last day had left this earth two days before mother and the other two days after. The friends were together again.

I had little fear of death before and none at all after mother left. This does not mean that I do not enjoy life to the full or encourage others to enjoy it in whatever way they think brings them satisfaction. I have only one proviso: nothing we do should be done with the intention to hurt others. As much as possible should be done in the hope that it will help people, not forgetting that we too are one of those "people".

In January 1991 Elizabeth went to visit her family in Brazil. She wanted to take her parents to Argentina where part of her father's family lived. I wanted to see some of my friends and family in Europe. We had both gone through a tense period and felt that we deserved some relaxation in the background we were accustomed to. Our love for each other was strong enough to know that we did not have to be in close physical proximity all the time. Though we found later that after two weeks' separation we missed each other too much for a comfortable existence.

During our research into parapsychological phenomena we had

encountered "instrumental transcommunication" from energies, in some cases one may call them spirits, via instruments such as the telephone, tape recorder, radio, television and computers.

The first person I had met personally who was recently involved in the phenomena was Ken Webster. He describes his experiences in a book called *The Vertical Plane*. He was a teacher who occasionally brought a computer home over the weekend. At first he experienced some very powerful poltergeist activity in his cottage. Later he found messages on his computer which when printed out seemed to come from somebody who lived in the fifteenth century. Later he found that he could ask this entity questions and provided he was not in the room in which the computer stood he would get answers. Sometimes if he left a pen and paper on the computer the "entity" would give answers in handwriting. An analysis of the style, words used and handwriting indicated that it could indeed have been written in the fifteenth century.

On my trip to Europe this time I visited Martin Wenzel, a telecommunication engineer in Aachen, who had been studying instrumental transcommunication and other phenomena not easily explained by currently known physical theory.

Martin though retired is a very active and agile person to whom, as to me, some "knowledge" started coming well before we even understood the word "parapsychology". He is a "religious" person in the sense that he believes in God but does not necessarily go frequently to church or think that one religion is better than another.

An experiment which impressed me greatly consisted of focusing a video camera onto a television screen and connecting it by closed circuit to that TV. Once the video camera and the TV were running the resulting picture on the screen would be recorded by a VCR. Thereafter the tape produced by the VCR could be viewed frame by frame, a tedious process, but some frames would show fairly clearly faces of people who were no longer physically alive, sometimes just friends or relatives who would be recognised by a surviving friend, but sometimes also famous people known to everybody through the media.

Very rarely a whole sequence of frames lasting many seconds when played at normal speed would appear showing a distinct event. Unfortunately this and many other such events are not reproducible. They will not occur when "asked" to occur. Many therefore say that they are scientifically not valid and either reject them or "forget" them.

When I talk about these experiences some people will simply leave the room, feel that they have to go to the toilet, make themselves some coffee or go for a walk. They simply do not wish to be exposed to something their conscious mind cannot easily explain.

I have now learned to stop talking about such matters with people who "do not wish to know". I may mention them again many months later. Sometimes there is a very positive reaction and they want to know more. Sometimes I am met again with a blank stare and I stop.

The reactions seem to have little, if anything, to do with a person's knowledge of science, history, literature or general education. Although people at a very high level of education or those who have practically no formal education seem to be less likely to react with complete rejection.

"Tadek, I miss you. How are things with you?" It was Elizabeth's voice over the telephone from Argentina.

"I am fine. I have met Martin Wenzel, a fascinating person. When I showed him your photograph he said he knew you."

"Impossible," she answered and then added, "but nothing is impossible. If he said he knew me he might mean he knew me from another plane. Right now I am worried. My mother is not well. The doctor does not know what is wrong with her. I am taking her back to Brazil."

"I shall now go to Mucke, then to Professor Senkowski who has written a book on transcommunication and then come back to Edo my cousin. Ring me once you know what is happening with your mother. I love you. Any time you feel I should come to São Paulo I can fly over the next day."

I drove first to Mucke in Heidelberg, my "oldest" girlfriend, with whom I always shared my thoughts and experiences. Just by talking with her my thoughts became often more focused and certainly her presence, even just her house, relaxed me. She is a petite girl yet when one is in her presence one has the feeling of a powerful woman. It is not her mode of speech nor the timbre of her voice. It is something deeper. One feels comfortable in her presence. I am not the only one to have this feeling. To me it is now another example of an energy, an "aura", that people emit.

"I have come across 'Instrumental Transcommunicatiori'. Have you heard of it?"

"I think I know what you mean, but explain. There is a department of parapsychology at the University of Freiburg. I have read some of their publications, but know little about what you call 'Instrumental Transcommunication'. Tell me more about it."

"You know that some mediums on occasion speak in a voice which is not their normal voice and which sometimes claims to be the spirit of a person who died or that of an energy that has never been part of a human being. Rosemary Brown, an English lady still alive, started composing music which was indistinguishable from Liszt and later other pieces from other composers who had died. In her book called *Unfinished Symphony* she describes how first one and then the other composers who were no longer alive came to her, dressed usually in clothes which she imagined were used during their lifetime, and asked her to compose pieces which they had no time to write during their lifetime. Under their 'inspiration' she wrote the notes they asked her to write. She had not composed anything before this 'inspired' composing started. Either she is a genius able to compose in the various styles of other composers or what she says is true. Records of her music are available.

"In instrumental transcommunication the 'disincarnated entities' or energies pass their words to living people through instruments.

"The first clear description of this phenomenon is when a Swede who liked taping the sound of birds in fields and forests found that superimposed on the bird sounds were human-sounding voices. This occurred frequently, though he could hear no human voices with his ears.

"Later, after the Second World War, when a film was being made on wartime airfields, the voices of pilots in their planes whilst on missions during the war appeared on the film crews' tapes.

"Sometimes the telephone rings and a voice claiming to be that of an 'entity' introduces himself. There were cases when this voice asked for the radio to be tuned to a certain wavelength, where no station normally broadcasts at a certain time. Near the appointed time one or more voices started speaking. Pictures appeared on TV sets and in one well-described and documented case messages came through the computer. Sometimes on new blank tapes sounds appeared, often clear sentences, purporting to come from other than human sources.

"Much of what one hears about these matters is probably made up, but some is, I feel certain, true and I intend to research it more in greater depth."

"Yes," she replied, "I suppose nothing is impossible. I know several doctors who use Kirlian photography, in particular photographs of the aura of the hand or finger tips, to help them with their diagnosis. I know some people say they can see the aura; it certainly shows on photographs."

This attitude was in complete contrast to that taken by my cousin Edo who, like many others, but fortunately a decreasing number, maintain that what is not reproducible or explicable by today's scientific methods cannot be taken seriously. Usually they do not wish to think or speak about it.

There is yet a third category amongst my friends. They feel that there may well be something to many of the currently inexplicable phenomena, but since however hard they try they can find no explanation for them, and indeed find that in some cases these phenomena are bogus, they have periods when they prefer to think only of the three-dimensional reality. Then, sometimes, for no particular reason, they go through a period when they are certain that there is more to life than we are taught in school, and indeed more than many religious people proclaim. Some of them are highly educated and are themselves surprised at their variation in attitude. It is as though they wanted to believe that there is something more to our existence than the purely physical aspect, but something is holding them back from doing so.

After two days' rest in Mucke's house I drove to Mainz where Professor Senkowski's wife received me with snacks consisting of delicious German sausage on black rye bread. Soon Ernst Senkowski arrived and took me to his study.

A fascinating person, in his early sixties, who wrote what was then considered the "bible" of instrumental transcommunication, he demonstrated to me, amongst others, one of the most interesting phenomena in this field.

The radio was tuned to a certain wavelength and a voice started speaking. At first it sounded mechanical like that of a toy robot, then after about half a minute it became more fluent and "human-like" as though it had to get used to speaking correctly. Then came the most surprising aspect. The voice would answer questions put to it. Of course if one insists on being a sceptic one could assume that there was somewhere a hidden microphone, somebody heard the questions and answered them through a transmitter. Senkowski was far too intelligent and serious to either manufacture or be taken in by such tricks. He himself described to me cases where he suspected trickery.

It is interesting that nearly all cases of instrumental transcommunication are observed by scientists. Is it because most belonging to this group of humanity can only be convinced that there are energies, other than those we can measure, by observing them through instruments?

"Mediumistic Transcommunication" on the other hand occurs usually, but by no means always, through people who are not highly academically educated and will, therefore, accept such a phenomenon with less resistance.

Yet even in cases of instrumental transcommunication the contact between whatever or whoever it is, and the recipient, seems to be easier if somebody who has mediumistic potential is present.

My present theory is that the spirit or energy which wishes to communicate with us acts like a transmitter and the medium is a receiver. The transmitter must transmit on a wavelength to which the receiver can be or is tuned. In addition the medium must also be able to act as a focus on which the transmitter can concentrate. Some people become mediums spontaneously while others might have been so as children but have been told so frequently that they are talking nonsense or imagining things that they "switched off" that part of themselves which was the receiver.

Many of us can probably become mediums if we are prepared to "turn down" the everyday problems and permit ourselves to be relaxed and open. Above all, we must try and switch off all doubt in the reality of transcommunication. If we decide to do this we must also protect ourselves, and I shall write more about this later. Some maintain that if we open ourselves we can invite low-level spirits and become what is often called "possessed", but that can be avoided if we "protect" ourselves.

The hours spent with Professor Senkowski were fascinating. From our conversation I learned that among persons working in parapsychological, metaphysical or spiritual fields, or whatever one might wish to call them, there are as many people with personal ambitions, dislikes and even lack of responsibility as people working in other fields. On the other hand I found that there is a greater proportion who have high ideals, show a high degree of responsibility and try to do good for their fellow humans than amongst those who do not accept the existence of spirits or higher energies or simply the fact that things happen which our orthodox knowledge is incapable of explaining.

After I returned to my cousin Edo, Elizabeth telephoned from São Paulo.

"The news is not good. They think that my mother has malignant cancer. She does not know it. They are giving her painkillers but say it is not operable."

Elizabeth never makes things appear worse than they are. She loved her mother intensely. I knew it was hard on her.

"How long do they think she will be with us?"

"Oh, several months. They do not know."

In a way I was glad they had put it that way. To tell a patient he has three months to live is frequently in my opinion equivalent to telling him, "Make sure you live no more than three months." His trust in doctors is such that he will die in three months. On the other hand I believe, as is now usually done in England, in telling him the truth, namely that he has cancer, without using the word "terminal" or specifying a time limit.

The knowledge of one's illness gives one the chance to fight it in ways the medical profession cannot. One can mobilise one's inner forces by whatever technique one feels comfortable with. Some will just concentrate or meditate in their own way. Some will resort to natural remedies or vitamins. It is their own will to live which may well be the main cause of a remission. Some may, and I know such cases, go on a prolonged fast for up to twelve weeks and then stay on a vegetarian diet, using vegetables on which no chemical sprays or artificial fertilisers have been used. Many lose all symptoms of cancer and even the growth itself.

When I discussed this with orthodox doctors, many said that the remission could not possibly have anything to do with the above "treatment". In fact, they thought it was wrong to use such "treatment" because there was no reason why it should work and patients might refuse orthodox treatment. This I found puzzling since the orthodox diagnosis was "a terminal case" of three months or perhaps a little longer. When told of the high rate of remission achieved when orthodox treatment seemed to have little effect, their answer was that the sample on which these statements was based was too small to be significant. In recent years, however, I met some who changed their mind after being confronted by too many "miraculous" remissions following alternative methods, sometimes in conjunction with orthodox treatment.

There are many "healers" who "lay on hands" which simply means that the healer holds his hands close to the patient and causes as yet immeasurable healing energies to focus on the patient. There are many well-documented cases where this technique caused remission of cancer or stopped its development. Mathew Manning in England was one such healer who was thoroughly investigated by scientists and journalists. The results were published in the *Manchester Guardian* and elsewhere. To anybody who does not block from his mind the knowledge which he finds uncomfortable for one reason or another, this and other articles should prove that there is something in this mode of healing as well, even though we do not understand it.

An increasingly large group of doctors are beginning to accept that there is more to healing than the knife and chemicals. Acupuncture, which was laughed at a decade ago, is now fully accepted, though the mode by which it acts is not understood. It is accepted that stress is the cause of many illnesses and that stress relief is an important factor in the cure of a patient. Homeopathic medicines are so highly diluted that in a spoonful there may not be a single molecule of the original "active" ingredient left. If they do have an effect then it can only be as a result of the "energy" or "information" left in the solvent. This too is inexplicable by current scientific knowledge.

Many doctors who graduated in orthodox medicine and practised it for a time have decided to use homeopathic techniques, frequently combined with herbs.

Some doctors who practise orthodox medicine on the National Health Service in England have a healer in their surgery once a week, and discuss cases with him if the patient permits it. Indeed the patient may wish to be treated by the healer. Some major hospitals in England will permit and even call healers to come to patients if they so wish, but others will not.

Philippa Puller once organised a workshop which was led by David Cousins who seemed to me a highly interesting person. Not only was he able to "induce" in people deeper thoughts about the purpose of their life and to cause some to be healed, but he also had some clairvoyant ability. How much I did not at the time know and anyway I did not believe in absolute clairvoyance, only in probabilities which some might see. I felt David was an exceptional person and decided to drive down to his home near Cardiff in Wales.

David had been a simple milkman and at that time unknown by most who worked in spiritual or metaphysical fields. His home, though meticulously clean, was simple. His wife received me and after she offered me a cup of tea David appeared. He was of medium height, unimposing, but warm and extremely charming. His depth was not immediately apparent, but after he spoke for a period of time one realised that he talked "under guidance".

David took me to his garage which he had converted into a study, put a microphone round his neck, switched on a tape recorder and spoke. His speech was rapid and often punctuated by a brief amiable smile. Frequently he spoke so quickly that I found it difficult to understand him; he had no hesitation in repeating or explaining anything if asked to do so, yet I felt that it broke his flow and only asked if I felt that the context of what he said was too difficult for me to understand.

I had had many incarnations before. I did not really need this one. I chose to come because I felt that I wanted to teach something, yet I was still asleep and just beginning to wake up. A group of spirits were waiting for me to wake up fully so that they could work through me if I permitted them to do so. Once this happened there would be dramatic changes in my life. I would do at last what I came to do. My life was important; it would help in development. Some spirits in particular were waiting with impatience for me to wake up. I was part of a plan but of course I had my free will.

He mentioned the time when I would reach certain stages, know more of my past and know the choices available for my future. All this to me at the time was a little confusing. I wondered what would happen when I "woke up". Would I be different in any way? In time I forgot most of what David had said or at least I thought I had.

Chapter 9

Some years later I met Trigueirinho, a well-known Brazilian writer in the esoteric field, because I wanted to discuss with him the future of the world, which he had written about.

He said to me, "Work in Brazil or Europe or anywhere you like. You will not go wrong. You have given permission to an elevated 'group of spirits' to work through you. So do what you want to do. It will be right, but do it quickly. There is not much time."

Was it the same group David Cousins had talked about?

Six months after Trigueirinho I met Douglas Forbes, a South African clairvoyant, whilst he was visiting London. After he realised that I knew that dramatic changes would soon occur on our globe he said, "You have been guided. You have sown your seeds correctly. Your work is in Brazil. This is where you and your centre will help during the transition in the near future. You will soon stay there for several years."

This saddened me, since though I love Brazil I also love Europe and like returning to it frequently. It reminded me also of a dream which my mother had in 1947 when we were living in England.

In this dream, she saw a big white statue and clearly heard the words, "This is your port." At the time she thought it was the Statue of Liberty outside New York and that we would emigrate to the USA. Indeed, years later I was offered a professorship in California. After initially accepting it, I rejected it to the great surprise of many friends.

Later, when I first came to Brazil in 1987, I sent mother a card from Rio de Janeiro on which was the town's symbol, an enormous white figure of Christ standing on a hill in the outskirts of Rio. There are many such statues of Christ, though smaller, near other towns in Brazil.

When mother received this card she wrote back saying, "It is this statue that I saw in my dream forty years ago, not the Statue of Liberty."

Did she then see that I would do my most important work in Brazil? That I would marry a Brazilian? Are all these visions part of the same All-Pervasive Energy?

After the telephone call from Elizabeth, telling me about her mother's illness, I drove back to London and telephoned her. "I shall come in two days. Find out what your mother would like to do and let's do it. Whatever time is left to her in this life let us make it as enjoyable as possible. Sometimes doctors can be wrong."

"I hope you are right. It is difficult. Come soon."

When I arrived Elizabeth collected me from the airport. In London it had been near freezing. In São Paulo it was midsummer and 40° C at noon, a contrast which is quite a shock for the organism. I bought Elizabeth a rose at the airport, as I had always done. To me she was now, as she had been since I remembered her again three and a half years ago, the most important person in my life. Every time I see her an indescribable feeling of joy goes through my whole body, a joy I feel in both my stomach and my head, or as some would say in my solar plexus and my third eye area.

"I love you."

"I have missed you," came the answer.

"How is mother?"

"So far, happy as always. She has no pain. She seems content. How much longer?"

When we arrived home nothing seemed to have changed, yet the atmosphere in the flat seemed to be different.

Orthodox medicine gave no hope. She was given painkillers. Sometimes, certainly not always, alternative methods can help. Since her family did not want to tell her that she had cancer, the possibilities were limited.

Someone knew an orthodox priest who had helped in several "hopeless" cases. Because of his healing abilities, his fellow priests thought that many of the parishioners came to his church just because he was there, so he was removed from his church. He was an unusually sensitive person. He did not give much hope for mother's recovery. He came several times but never charged for his visits. He liked Elizabeth and whenever he said goodbye to me he whispered, "You have a good energy."

Some people, even some doctors, seem to leave behind them a heavy atmosphere in the house which they have visited, while others leave behind a feeling of hope even though they have not expressed it in words; not hope that what one wants to happen will happen but just hope, a knowledge, that there is something good somewhere not too far away. He was one of the latter category.

Elizabeth's mother had always been the centre of the family. Every

Thursday some or all of the children, grandchildren, cousins, nephews, nieces and some close friends came for lunch, a mixture of Italian and Arabic dishes - her husband was born in Italy and she was of Lebanese descent. There might be twelve people at the table or there might be twenty or more. One never knew. It was a time when news was exchanged, the atmosphere of togetherness refreshed and help given or obtained if required.

Some came at noon or even before and some a little later. Lunch started promptly at 1 pm. Some left immediately after lunch; some stayed longer, particularly if there were important items to be discussed. All were selfemployed so they could make the time. It reminded me of the times when I was a child in Poland. There it was Sunday when the whole family and many friends came for lunch, in the beautiful garden if the weather was good, or in the large dining room if it rained and in winter.

The atmosphere created during such a meeting can be not only harmonious but also very healing. People leave with a feeling that whatever their personal difficulties and whatever unpleasant things may be happening around them, the world is beautiful and it is up to us to perceive this beauty. However difficult things may appear to be, we can experience a contentedness within ourselves if we so wish and believe that whatever is happening may well be for the best. If it had not happened perhaps something else that was worse might have occurred. Just as with my accident, which caused me so much pain, the prospect of never being able to walk again and to think clearly eventually resulted in my being a person more content and happy than I believed a human being could be.

It was during one of those Thursday lunches that we agreed to concentrate on mother every day at noon wherever we might be and say the prayer "Our Father". Concentrated thought of many people does have an effect. What the effect will be is difficult to say, for one can only pray and concentrate that what is best for the person should happen. We do not always know what the best is. What is the point of keeping a person alive if he or she has experienced all that was necessary, and by living longer may suffer more at a later stage.

There may be a "plan" for all of us but we also have a free will which can modify this plan. If there was no free will we would be machines which most of us believe we are not.

Olga, Elizabeth's mother, was still an agile person who wanted to see more of the world and, perhaps most importantly, gave a lot to her family by gently holding it together, giving love and help to all around her. I hoped that by passing to her some of our energy, it would be used to heal her and that this was what was best for her.

"I have wanted a better shower in our bathroom for quite some time now. Do you think you could do something about it?" she asked Elizabeth.

"It should not be too difficult."

We found one that could be used as a replacement and had it fitted.

"I want to go down to our flat on the beach, but there is also a spa where the waters are supposed to be healthy and a hotel in which all treatments are concentrated - very beautiful in the south of Brazil - I would like to go there as well."

We went first for a weekend to the beach where she had a flat. She loved the sea. We took long walks along the beach. She was perfectly happy.

Perhaps our prayers or perhaps the priest's healing was working. Perhaps her life span would be extended. Life continued as before, except that all of us concentrated on Olga at noon every day.

She had never liked the settee in the TV room. It looked fine but was uncomfortable, so we spent several days looking at other settees but could not find anything suitable.

Easter was approaching.

"Let's have a really glorious Easter."

"How about renting a large house in the country where not only the family but many friends could come and help celebrate."

"That would be lovely, but can we find something large enough? There may be twenty or thirty people."

Everybody started looking. A house with a swimming pool, tennis courts and an enormous garden was found. At least a dozen children would be there, so Elizabeth bought a hundred balloons and innumerable other items with which we were going to decorate the house for Easter Sunday.

People started arriving on Thursday. Friday to Saturday was a continuous party. I remember getting completely worn out on Saturday evening, blowing up balloons after the children had gone to bed, whilst Elizabeth and a friend were sticking them and other items to the wall. Some were swimming in the pool; someone nearly broke a leg when she slipped on the wet marble floor. One or two admired the clear night sky whilst others were putting the finishing touches to the feast that was to be consumed on Sunday.

Bang! Bang! Bang!

"What is happening? Bandits? A Revolution?"

The former is not an infrequent occurrence in Brazil.

"No, no," Elizabeth answered. "Just the children sticking pins into the balloons."

It was a gloriously sunny Easter Sunday. The spirit of "togetherness" was beautiful. We all ate a little too much. Some of us drank a little more than was healthy, but all were supremely happy. The house though very large did not have enough beds for all of us, so some had to sleep on the floors. It did not worry any of us. After a hilarious day we all had an excellent night. Mother in particular was happy to have the whole family, especially the smaller children, around her. Things looked good.

After we returned to São Paulo mother asked, "What have they done to me when I was last in hospital? I feel a pressure or pain inside me."

"Probably something small," Elizabeth answered. "We shall take you to hospital and they will examine you again."

They decided to anaesthetise her. Hours later she woke up. Her heartbeat became irregular. Then her breathing became difficult. She was taken into the intensive care unit. Soon the whole family gathered in the waiting room. We took it in turn to look at her through a window so positioned that she too could see the person looking at her. At a certain stage I had to go to the bathroom.

When I returned Elizabeth said, "Her spirit has left her."

For a moment there was absolute silence, then she said, "Let us pray for her. May her spirit find its passage to its proper place easily. It is a good spirit. Our Father who art..."

It was the 28th April 1991 and only just four months after my mother had died. None of us had expected it so soon. Her heart had simply given up for no good reason. Why? My answer was that she was not meant to experience real pain or the indignity of living in a drugged state. It was better that way. It was easy for me to say this. I had sat by my mother's bedside when she died and held my father's hand when he passed away. Both had suffered before this final moment. I had seen others of my family die. I had had time to realise that death is only a graduation to a different level.

For Elizabeth my mother's death four months ago was the first she had witnessed. A second death so little time later, and that of the person she loved most, was going to be a great shock when she had had time to fully realise what had happened.

For twenty-four hours she would not have time for anything but technicalities. In Brazil they have a custom of having the funeral twenty-four hours after the death. This day is called the velorio. One or more of the closest family sit near the body all the time and accept condolences. Another member of the family informs all relatives and friends where the velorio is. As soon as people hear of it they come, usually in their working clothes because there may be no time to go home and change. Some come from a hundred, some from a thousand or more miles away. They go to the airport straight from the office. Elizabeth's elder sister was in Argentina, somewhere between two appointments at the time. Even the police were asked to help in finding her.

A hundred or was it two hundred people came. Some stayed half an hour and some many hours. Some were quiet with tears in their eyes while others were more vocal. Elizabeth's father sat there as though it had nothing to do with him. He was stunned. Only once did he scream. He complained bitterly.

"Why didn't anybody tell me that she had cancer and that she was going to die?"

"We told you immediately after it was confirmed," his son answered.

"No, I knew nothing about it."

This explained why throughout her illness he had behaved as though there was nothing wrong with her. He had simply put a block between the truth, which he did not want to accept, and his conscious mind.

Elizabeth's elder sister arrived from the airport under police escort when the coffin was being closed.

As in the case of my mother we were again in the first car behind the hearse. As with my mother it was afternoon and we were driving in a westerly direction into a beautiful sunset. In my mind I saw both spirits going into the light. As physical beings they were both charming, good and loved by all those near them, yet very different. As spirits they were both highly elevated and probably similar.

Father - I always called him father though he was my father-in-law; I had lost mine more than ten years ago and suppose it was a sign of my love and respect for him - pretended nothing had happened. The most he said was, "It had been so long that we were together."

We suggested he sell his flat and move into a flat literally next door to his youngest daughter. It had just come onto the market.

He looked at it, but then said, "Here I know where I am." And that was it.

How would he take the loss of his wife? How long would he live? As long as we were there he had company. But when we returned to England? He had two more daughters and a son, but they had their own lives to lead. He would be much of the time alone.

To make the transition easier we suggested we would drive him through Paraguay to Argentina where much of his family lived.

The drive from São Paulo to Foz de Iguacu on the border of Paraguay takes two days. We had seen Foz de Iguacu and its waterfalls, perhaps the most beautiful in the world, before. From there we tried to cross to the other side of the river into Ciudad del'Este in Paraguay.

At the border the official who looked at my passport said, "You are illegally in Brazil. Your visa has expired. You will have to pay a fine. Perhaps they will extend your visa."

"But my husband has been here for less than three months. A visa is valid for three months."

My Portuguese was very poor so Elizabeth did most of the talking for me.

"Well, usually it is, but the official entered thirty days when your husband landed in São Paulo."

"Where do we go to extend the visa?"

"To the police station in Foz de Iguacu."

We turned round and found the police station. After waiting an appropriate time, we were shown into an office and told again that I was illegally in Brazil and must therefore pay a fine.

"All right, how much is the fine? I shall make out a cheque right now.

Can you give him a new visa?"

"No, first you must go to a bank, pay the fine into an account which I shall give you, get a receipt, bring the receipt to me and then we can discuss a new visa."

We went to the bank; there was a long queue at the counter where fines were paid. An hour later we were back at the police station with the necessary receipt. Another half hour and I got a new visa, this time for the customary three months though I required it only for a day. We went back to the border and showed our passports to first the Brazilian and then to the Paraguayan authorities. All was in order. We drove on towards the capital.

The contrast in scenery was colossal. There were very few houses along the road, most of them in a semi-dilapidated state, very few cars and nearly all of them with non-Paraguayan registration numbers.

Some sixty miles down the road the police stopped us.

"Passports, please," they asked very politely. There was no problem with them.

"Car papers."

Elizabeth handed over the registration book.

"No! Car papers."

"Perhaps he means the insurance papers," I said to Elizabeth.

So she gave him the insurance papers and all other papers relating to the car.

"No, no! Car papers like car passport." The policeman became slightly irritated. "The one you got when you crossed the border."

"But we did not get anything when we crossed the border, just a stamp in my husband's passport," Elizabeth explained in Spanish. Without her knowledge of the language we would have been completely lost. I kept smiling. What else could I do? Never argue with the police in South America. Father sat in the back pretending to take no interest in the proceedings. He can switch off completely.

"Without a 'car passport' you cannot enter the country further than sixty kilometres from the border. Perhaps they thought at the border post you only wanted to go to the Ciudad del'Este. You should have told them that you wanted to go further."

"Sorry, how was I to know this? What do we do now?"

"Go back to the border."

Chapter 9

So we drove back.

Just before the border we started losing water from the radiator. There was no garage, of course, so we crossed back into Brazil and went to a garage. They could not repair the fault, so we went to another garage. Yes, they could repair it. Tomorrow it would be ready.

After a night in a hotel we decided that we were probably not meant to go to Paraguay, since we had been sent back twice.

Foz de Iguacu lies in a corner of Brazil bordering on both Paraguay and Argentina. In the morning after collecting the car we headed for Argentina this time.

At the border there was a long line of cars. When it was our turn to enter the country the border official just waved us on.

"My husband's passport is British," Elizabeth said. "I am sure he needs a visa stamp in his passport. Do my father and I not need a stamp as well? Anything required for the car?"

She was taking no chances this time.

"All right, go to this window there." He pointed impatiently at an official behind in a booth smoking a cigarette.

"He will know whether your husband needs a stamp and give it to you."

We both went with all the passports and car papers to the official indicated. He took my passport and stamped in a visa valid for a month, but took no interest in any of the other passports or car papers.

"That's all you need," was the only comment.

About thirty miles from the border a police car overtook us and waved us down.

"Passports, please," he politely asked with great dignity in his voice.

Elizabeth handed over the passports. He looked first at hers.

"When did you enter the country?"

"Oh, about an hour ago," she answered.

"There is no entry stamp in your passport. You entered illegally."

"But nobody wanted to see our passports. I had to insist that they put a visa stamp into my husband's passport; he is British. I felt sure he needed one, so they put one into his but not into mine."

"Well, they were wrong. Let me see your husband's passport. Yes, that seems all right."

As always, we smiled and asked, "What do we do now?"

"Ah well, just drive on. They are often very busy at the border and forget to stamp the passport."

We continued on our way. An hour or two later we were stopped again by a police car; again there was the same problem and again my visa saved us. It showed that we had not avoided the border control post. We were stopped twice more before we reached Buenos Aires and each time had the same conversation.

The Argentinians, though bordering on Brazil, are a very different people. They take themselves much more seriously. They speak and move with dignity. Driving through towns, especially Buenos Aires, one could see that once Argentina had been a very wealthy country.

The streets are wide and frequently lined with trees. The houses are well designed and obviously once very beautiful. There are large parks and beautiful monuments. But the paint is flaking off most houses, the streets are not clean and most public telephones do not work. I was told that the public administration is in complete chaos.

Obviously the citizens were once a proud people who designed their towns and shops to compete with the best one finds in Europe. There is even a branch of Harrods in Buenos Aires. To me their capital is a mixture of Paris and pre-war Warsaw, with parks and golf courses resembling those found in England. Now they are obviously poor, though they have retained much of their pride, and are unable to keep up what they once created.

I have heard it frequently said that the Argentinians are Italians who speak Spanish and pretend to be English. There is some truth in this.

On the other hand, the way their country looks reminded me of some of the most beautiful towns in central and eastern Europe, which used to have imposed upon them a communist regime, with its associated bureaucratic incompetence resulting in economic decline. For example, Krakow in Poland, a beautiful thousand-year-old town, with the second oldest university in Europe, now dirty, facades of houses in disrepair, and parks not looked after.

This is rapidly changing in all the ex-communist European countries, particularly since they became real democracies. One can but hope that the same change will occur in Argentina and that it will return to its former glory. For this to happen a very enlightened government would have to be in power.

CHAPTER 10

Brazil, the Country of the Future
Brazil has the seed but does not know it.

I personally feel that Brazil, though it has never been as beautiful as Argentina from an architectural point of view, and is in as great an economic mess as most South American countries, is a country that is awake, spiritually rather than economically, whilst other countries, including European and North American, are still asleep or just beginning to awake. All it requires are more teachers to give it a firm direction.

It is like a large school full of children but very few teachers. The children are bright, charming, full of good intentions but inexperienced in worldly matters.

They have lots of inner guides but many of them are too slow and some a little polluted.

There is much good energy in Brazil but also some which is holding it back. Most politicians, even if they start with good intentions, seem to be drawn immediately into an egocentric field and try to improve only their own financial position, not that of their country. They act as if they were possessed and will not listen to reason or even follow what instinct told them before they were elected to their office. They will not accept that they and their families would be better off if all families earned a reasonable wage. They refuse to accept that because of their bureaucracy and low wages everything is twice as expensive as in most other countries.

Unfortunately it is not only their politicians but also many of their top businessmen who have the same attitude.

Yet many realise that things will change. Some think it is a matter of dozens of years, while others are more positive and hope that great changes will occur in a very few years. They realise that inspiration obtained outside, in other countries, is valuable, because inside Brazil one is held back; too many people try to manipulate you and give you a hard time. That is why foreigners are treated in Brazil as people to look up to and as people who can do things better.

This is not true. It is the Brazilians who on the whole are brighter than most others once they start believing in themselves. This seems to be easier when they are outside their own country or spend some time abroad. In spite of comparatively little financial support from the state, Brazil has more world-class athletes than most other countries. Some of the top surgeons in many fields, including plastic surgery, eye surgery and heart surgery, are Brazilians. Brazilian engineers build good roads when on contract abroad, but extremely poor roads when in their own country. They work fast and well in hotels abroad, but slowly and unreliably when in Brazil.

It is the country's mentality which has to change to a new pattern. The solar plexus energy and the sexual energy have to go to a higher level. More "heart operations" are required to replace some of the occult and shamanistic work, however beautiful shamanism can be elsewhere. I believe this will happen very soon.

I believe that they will realise sooner than most others that we all manipulate energy and that this can be good and necessary, and that they must learn to manipulate this energy correctly. The number of people trying to hurt others by occult means is still large, but I believe that it is rapidly diminishing. On the other hand the number of people working with heart energy is increasing.

North America, which the Brazilians consider a paradise, does not give me that impression of rapid spiritual evolution, and neither does Argentina, the country through which we were now travelling. The people may appear to be prouder and perhaps more adult, but they have lost the spirit of childhood. They are not the children to whom the future belongs. They do not give the impression of a people who "have the seed but do not know it".

After having visited all of father's relatives, where we were royally entertained, we decided to return to Brazil by ferry and via Uruguay.

When we arrived at the port the immigration officials stated quite simply, "You have no entry stamp in your passport so you are not here. Therefore, you cannot leave."

Elizabeth explained again that I had a stamp, but nobody wanted to

144

stamp her and her father's passports.

"That is not my fault. You will be fined and then we shall see what happens."

We were sent to another office. There the official was a little more understanding.

"You will pay US $100 fine and I can then give you an entry stamp. After that you will be able to leave."

It was good that we had arrived a long time before the departure of the ferry, as otherwise we would have had to wait until the next morning's ferry.

The car ferry was extremely comfortable; we had a superb night and an excellent breakfast. On arrival in Uruguay we were not going to take any chances. We asked to be shown to the port's main immigration office, explained our past troubles and insisted on big fat stamps in our passports.

Uruguay, though ethnically very similar to Paraguay and mainly a mixture of Red Indians and the Spanish invaders, developed in a completely different way. The people are on the whole very polite; the towns are clean and the roads are good. There is not the obvious difference between the rich and the poor. One could be anywhere in central or western Europe.

We took a guided bus tour of the city where the guide was supposed to give a commentary amongst other languages in English. Since I was the only one who did not speak Spanish she asked Elizabeth to translate for me. She did not ask politely but simply stated that that was the way it was going to be.

Elizabeth, after having told me that the Uruguayans are an extremely polite and well-mannered people, felt let down. So when we returned to our hotel she told the hotel manager of the incident. He telephoned the tour company running the sight-seeing tours and the next morning the guide, whom Elizabeth had taken offence to, came to the hotel, apologised to us and returned all our tour fees. They are a polite and respectful people. They give the appearance of maturity, but to me they are not the children who "have the seed".

It is interesting how very different the people in the various South American countries are.

Brazil, by far the largest, was conquered by the Dutch in the north and the Portuguese in the south. The Dutch were beaten by the Portuguese. Some, but few, remained. All the other parts of South America were conquered mainly by the Spaniards, though a vast number of Italians emigrated to Argentina later, but many also to Brazil and other parts. Very many Syrians and Lebanese emigrated to Brazil, but some to other South American countries. Poles, Germans, some Russians and other Europeans emigrated mainly during this century to the various parts of South America. There are whole towns whose inhabitants are of predominantly Polish or German descent with schools in which those languages are taught. The official language in Brazil is Portuguese and everywhere else Spanish, though Paraguay and one or two countries also have their own language derived from an Indian base.

Essentially they are all a mixture of Europeans, mainly Spanish or Portuguese and Indians with a large influx of Negroes particularly in Brazil. One would expect them to have many similar characteristics, yet they are very different. The only similarities are unstable governments and high inflation rates.

There is one very essential and to me significant difference between Brazil and the rest. All Brazilian revolutions were practically bloodless, whereas in other countries vast numbers died. During one Brazilian revolution, so I was told, a colonel walked into the president's office and said, "Sir, I think you ought to resign."

"Why should I?" the president responded.

"Look out through the window and you will see."

Outside there was a company of soldiers with their guns aimed at the president.

"I take your point," the president said and signed the resignation form given to him by the colonel. No blood was spilled.

Why should people of such similar hereditary backgrounds be so very different? Even the average climate of Brazil and many Central or South American countries is not so very different.

The Brazilians may speak loudly, as most Mediterranean and Latin American people do, but they are not aggressive. They are capable of working very hard, and do so with pleasure when given the right leadership. They are not fanatical in political and religious aspects. They are in general extremely hospitable and a happy people, capable of extreme

146

expressions of togetherness and gaiety as shown in their carnivals. They do not attack their neighbours and try not to get involved in wars. They not only believe in but practise freedom of speech. The Roman Catholic church may be the predominant church, but many Roman Catholics are also espírita, that is they believe in the existence of spirits who can speak through people and heal. There are Orthodox Catholics, Protestants, Jews and Moslems. I have never heard of any of them speaking badly of the others.

It is true that there is much lawlessness including murder, and that there are many apparently irresponsible people there. I feel this to be so because of the lack of good responsible leadership for which the people are searching.

Nowhere in industrialised countries, and Brazil is industrialised and has a reasonable infrastructure when compared with Jordan, India, China or most of the African countries, is there such a large proportion of people who believe that there is more to life than the physically measurable aspects. Nowhere do so many people, from the least to the most educated, believe in and practise spiritual values other than just going to church on Sunday. In fact a smaller proportion go to church on Sundays than in many other predominantly Catholic countries. On the other hand very many go to various spiritual gatherings during the week and discuss what there is outside the three-dimensional life we all know about, and indeed what more there is to life and death than the average priest talks about during a Sunday service.

The poor in Brazil are very poor when compared with Europe or North America, but they are becoming a little better off. The minimum wage though low is increasing, whereas the difference between the poor and the wealthy in most other industrialised countries is increasing. All this contributes to my certainty that in a short time the seed in Brazil will suddenly start budding and blooming.

Father eats vast quantities of fruit. Wherever we were he bought them by the boxful. He consumes a pound or more early in the morning before his shower. Now he lost his fruit knife - a minor tragedy. Whilst in the restaurant he saw a knife of appropriate dimensions on the floor. He bent down, picked it up and let it disappear in his jacket sleeve. I opened my mouth and closed it again.

When I caught up with Elizabeth I said, "Father has just robbed a knife."

"Sh! Not so loud! He will always give when somebody is in need as you know. Now he is in need. He needed a fruit knife!"

Give and take is a typical attitude of so many. Father gives much more than he takes. He does not fire employees when they are too old to be efficient. Many others still take more than they give, but this too I feel is changing. Lectures on this and associated subjects, on the correct form of living, whether with a spiritual or psychological bias, are frequently completely sold out, particularly when given by people who come from outside Brazil.

The next night we spent in a hotel on the coast. Elizabeth and I chose a chalet facing the sea. The sandy beach started right outside the door. I love the sound of breaking waves. Father chose a more civilised room inside the main building. He and I arranged to meet in the sauna. Elizabeth does not like saunas. It was a mixed sauna. In Europe it is customary to be naked in mixed saunas; in Brazil it is not. This did not worry father, or more likely he just did not think. He usually does what he wants to do.

I came out from the changing room in swimming trunks; he was naked. Some ladies who came out from another cabin turned pointedly away. We entered first the dry sauna. As we did so several ladies walked out. After a shower we entered the steam room. Once the ladies realised there was a naked man amongst them, most left. Some enjoyed the sight. Father paid no attention to all this. His thoughts were obviously elsewhere. I had put my swimming trunks on to be on the safe side. I did not know what the custom was in Brazil. I was beginning to realise that I had done the right thing.

When we went to the shower again an attendant came with a pair of swimming trunks and very politely suggested father put them on. He looked at them and then shook his head.

"They are not mine."

"I know, but you may use them," came the polite answer.

"Why?" he asked. "Much healthier to have a sauna naked."

Then it began to dawn on him.

"Oh! You mean the ladies here. I didn't notice there were any."

Reluctantly he put on the swimming trunks. He had meant no harm -

just a case of absentmindedness.

After our return to São Paulo, father was as adamant as before that he did not want to move out of his flat. He started driving again to the beauty salon in the morning, and then came back for lunch and a nap, and returned again for an hour to what was once the famous Antoine Establishment. There was no real need for him to go, but he enjoyed it.

Elizabeth continued the tradition of the Thursday lunch, to which the whole family and many friends came. Elizabeth was rapidly taking the place of her mother in as far as becoming the centre of the family was concerned. It was her greatest concern. She wanted the family to remain the closely knit unit it had always been. There is little that is more beautiful than a family which shares the good and the hard times.

During the last speech I made before we returned to our house in London, I said, and meant it, "In memory of mother, and for the good of all of us, there will always be a Thursday when those who can will meet here. Brazil is the country of the future. Let this family be a family of the future."

CHAPTER 11

Where do We go from Here?
We all have the knowledge;
it is just a question of perceiving it.

In 1988 we felt that we wanted to create in as many countries as we could an annual conference-exhibition-festival, the main object of which would be to build bridges between orthodox and alternative medicine, the scientific and the parapsychological approach and perhaps most importantly between the consumer and the ecologist. For what good is it to have a healthy body, and even a sensible spirit in it, if we destroy our world, a world which can be so beautiful and in which we can learn so much.

Even those of us who believe not only in the existence of a spirit in every body, but also in the existence of this spirit outside the body once it is dead, a spirit which goes through a continuous learning process, know that this spirit can learn some things only when it is incarnated in a physical body; and for the body as we know it to exist, a world which can nourish this body must also exist.

We felt that there was a rapidly increasing number of people worldwide who took an interest in the unorthodox and the spiritual, and wanted not only to know more about it, but also wanted that those interested in the orthodox should cooperate with those interested in unorthodox phenomena.

What we had in mind was a regular event, featuring an exhibition of books, techniques and equipment in the field of complementary medicine, relaxation, spiritual healing, visualisation, colour healing, acupressure and so on, as well as discussions, lectures and workshops.

To start it we would of course need sponsorship if we did not want to rely mainly on saleable items such as crystals, foods, and new age "gadgetry" in general. Once the first event was held we knew that enough money would be generated to permit the event to spread rapidly. In Brazil, a professional event organiser was prepared to start this venture in São Paulo, but at the last moment he withdrew. A private individual who could have afforded to sponsor it decided that the energies moved by such an undertaking were more than she could cope with. In Krakow, Poland, both a radio station who put me on the air for an hour and a TV station were prepared to provide the accommodation for such an event and to publicise it, but some money would have to be initially provided from west European countries, since Poland was going through a financial crisis. But so was the west. Unexpected difficulties appeared constantly.

In early 1991 we were beginning to wonder whether perhaps this was something we were not supposed to do, or perhaps it should be modified. We were not the sort of people who gave up easily, but we had learned that if something was supposed to happen, help would come, often from most unexpected sources. If it was not supposed to happen, constant difficulties would present themselves.

We gave some lectures in Brazil and England and talked to many about parapsychological subjects. When in England, our house was constantly full of people from all over the world. Some just needed moral support, some wanted to meet other people and hoped we could effect the right introduction. Some, perhaps the majority, knew that there was something they had to learn, to find out about, to see, experience, and that we were the people who could help them to do so. There was "something" about us, they said. What this "something" was we were to realise only later when we were told that together we radiated an energy which caused people to think more clearly, which caused things to occur.

After I learned to see auras at first round trees and later around people as well, I realised that this "energy" was something very real. Presumably Elizabeth's and my energies were such that they caused a resonance effect in each other and thus their joint power was much greater than the sum of their separate powers. Rather as a high sound can cause a resonance effect in a wine glass or even a window, and thus cause it to break.

Most of us have probably had experiences which showed that the mere presence of a single person, who may have said very little, could cause decisions to be made, a deeper understanding to be obtained and even new ideas to be evolved. When we speak of a person as having charisma, it is usually assumed that he can use words well, but have we not all met people who say nothing but are distinctly charismatic?

Since we have been together there have never been more than two days during the year when we were alone in our house in London. It is not much different in Brazil, where we are considered by many to be catalysts. We cause things to happen.

Sometimes when we know that we have to relax away from all those who feel that they need us, we tell our guests, who always get a key to the house when they arrive, "Sorry, we have to go away for seven, ten, or fourteen days." We then go to a travel agent and ask, "What have you got for tomorrow, preferably cheap?" There is always something available. It is in this way that we went, amongst other places, to Tunisia, Egypt, and various parts of Europe.

Through our personal knowledge of people (and their addresses) who have had messages via instruments from "spirits" or "energies" which so far cannot be measured using existing physical instruments, we were instrumental in causing the first "Transcommunication Congress" to be organised. It happened in São Paulo under the auspices of the Spirita Medical Association of São Paulo.

It was fascinating to see how many scientists had experienced the receiving of communications from other than physical sources. We hoped this would become a regular event.

Later we proposed the formation, in as many countries of the world as possible, of groups who would discuss current and probable future problems facing a given country, continent or the world.

The basic idea was to form a group consisting of any or all of the following: an orthodox and a complementary medical practitioner, an ecologist and an economist, a scientist, a parapsychologist, a politician, possibly a spiritual person such as a priest, a technologist, an industrialist, and most importantly somebody who was part of or had good contacts in the media, somebody with connections in the publishing world and anybody else who was thought appropriate. Above all, members of the group would have to have a rapport with each other. The types of problems to be discussed would include the elimination of extreme poverty, co-operation between the employer and employee, decrease in working hours and in the number of unemployed, the cause of the various economic cyclic effects, types of energy production to cause least harm to

the environment, use of fertilisers, types of transportation, effect of spirituality, co-operation between the various churches, use of alternative or
complementary medicine, co-operation between orthodox and unorthodox
approaches, realisation that what is orthodox in one country is unorthodox
in another, and any other problems which might be felt to be important.

Economists, politicians, religious leaders and other professionals had
not come up with answers to many of today's economic, social, and political problems, perhaps because there were none, but more likely because
they looked at any given problem from one point of view: that of their profession.

Interdisciplinary groups, so we felt, would develop a "spirit" of their
own or an atmosphere of their own, and perhaps come up with useful
answers. If two or more groups in different parts of the world should come
up with an identical or similar answer to any given problem, then this
would be particularly significant. All groups would therefore have to be in
contact with each other particularly when they come to a conclusion how
to tackle a given problem. The frequency with which they met would be
left entirely up to them.

We discussed this with several people. Perhaps this was the beginning
of what has now come into existence: the "Instituto Atalanta".

"Let us rethink what we really ought to do and how we ought to go
about it," Elizabeth said to me some time in 1993.

"Somehow I feel, whatever others may say, that we are not using our
energy to the best advantage," I answered. "Everybody says that we are a
lovely, helpful couple, and that we do a lot of good. It is very flattering.
We help a lot of individuals, we try to solve some people's problems and
many know they can rely on us; but, I agree with you, I am certain there
is something more that we should do," I added in full agreement.

"Hmm, why don't you write a book? So many people have told you
you should; even mediums say that you will write one," said Elizabeth,
expressing the thought that had often gone through my mind.

"One mistake that we are making is to have too little time for ourselves. We need some time to be alone, just you and I, not a week or two
but at least several months, somewhere in the mountains or in a forest, far
away from civilisation, from pollution, from being constantly on call, and
not to feel continually responsible for someone. I think we need to feel the

influence of nature. I know that researching mediums and understanding why they are frequently right, but also frequently wrong, is interesting and perhaps important, but I feel that if I can relax I shall see some of the more important answers.

"I also know that the commandment 'Love your neighbour as you love yourself' is right, but we and most others seem to misunderstand it. They assume that you love yourself more than you love others. In our and probably in many other cases, the opposite is the truth. We find no time to love ourselves. We always think of others, and forget that we too are human and need relaxation, time for ourselves, and not always to say we can do this or that for us later but right now he or she needs our help or 'this' has to be done. We too are one of the 'he' or 'she'. If we collapse we shall not be able to do at all what we want to do and others seem to expect us to do. We have to learn to say 'no' and not always 'yes' to all requests. Then we will be able to do even more, though perhaps in a different way."

"Of course you are right. Others have told us the same," Elizabeth replied.

"They certainly have, but we have not taken much notice of it. When we go back to England this year, the remainder of the year will belong to us. Let us promise this to each other before it is too late."

I seem to have had a premonition or perhaps I was just very tired. I did not know in what way we would know what our path was to be. But I knew that we would know it if we could generate the will to slow down.

After we returned to England in March 1993, we went on a three-week car tour of Scotland. It was glorious to be away from the intensity generated by industrial surroundings, to feel that nothing was disturbing communication with nature.

I remembered what several mediums had told me: that when I died clinically after my accident, my spirit had left my body, and had been "reminded" what it promised to try and do during this incarnation. It was now time I did it, whatever it was. What was it that I was supposed to do? The only hint I got was that my life to this moment, my teaching and scientific career, had been a preparation for the real work I had promised that I would do. My coma and subsequent heavy drugging to prevent pain may have caused me to forget any experiences I had whilst clinically dead. But if I tried hard I would remember what I was supposed to do.

All I knew was that for many it was the everyday "little" things they did, the acts of kindness, of love, the giving of hope to one or two friends who were lost that mattered because these acts showed who you really were and that all this was important to mankind, and improved it, but that I was expected to do something more. What? All I knew was that if I stayed away from the everyday involvements it would somehow come to me.

Our love for each other was growing, if that was possible, if it had not already reached the peak that human beings can reach. The countryside was glorious, wild, often no houses visible for miles, birds slowly walking across the road as though it belonged to them and our car was an intruder that could wait.

Our hosts in bed-and-breakfast houses were invariably helpful, the rooms clean and the breakfasts so large that we could eat no lunch, just fruit and a piece of bread. In the evening we always chose to eat "bar suppers". They were invariably enormous and delicious. Certainly the atmosphere in a pub was for our present mood vastly superior to that in a restaurant.

I felt that we lived in an environment that had been "civilised" too rapidly. "Environmentalism" might well become a major religion or political party, particularly if many more "accidents" occurred and pollution increased. With the rate at which people died from illnesses which were previously unknown or less common, illnesses which an increasing number of orthodox doctors related to moral, physical or chemical stress, I began to feel with increasing conviction that people would realise that the acquisition of wealth and power was not the only, or even main, reason for our lives.

During our trip round Scotland we not only visited the remotest parts and some of the islands but also Findhorn, a community created by four families on a wild, windswept part of the mid-eastern coast of Scotland. Its beginning and history are quite extraordinary.

A few families unemployed at the time decided, some feeling they were guided, to park their caravans on a piece of land incapable of supporting the vegetation which would have been necessary if they were to live off it. The soil layer was thin and windswept, yet they planted vegetables and they grew there, in spite of the fact that experts told them that it was impossible for this to happen.

The community grew rapidly and became a haven for those who wanted to lead a peaceful and spiritual life and experience nature. Many stayed there for years and others just for days, or to attend a conference or workshop. Topics covered ranged from the spiritual-esoteric to the very practical indeed and "high brow" such as a conference on "Intuitive Leadership" attended by industrialists from Europe and the other side of the Atlantic, the southern and northern hemispheres.

We had heard of Findhorn some years ago and at times entertained in our house those who had attended conferences there. Though the last time we had met someone who had been there was three years prior to our visit, all said that the atmosphere there was conducive to deep deliberations and not only did they learn a lot but they felt a "positive energy" there. At that time I did not really know what was meant by a "positive energy". Nevertheless both Elizabeth and I felt it would be good to experience it.

The people we met there were pleasant and polite. Some were more helpful than others. We were shown a film of the development of the place, beautiful and touching, and had a good vegetarian lunch. Yet I, and later Elizabeth told me that she as well, though perhaps not quite so intensely, began to feel most uncomfortable. After several hours we felt we had to leave. I had for the first time in my life felt a deeply depressing atmosphere. It was not anything that anybody had said or done. Was that what a "negative atmosphere" felt like? I had never experienced anything like it before. Since then I have become more sensitive and experienced similar feelings several times. It took many miles of driving through beautiful countryside before I felt my normal self again.

We discussed this phenomenon with several people including sensitives in the months that followed. Many felt that Findhorn was passing through a "bad patch" or trough. Somehow it had lost its direction, a phenomenon which happened in many communities.

More recently we heard from several people that the atmosphere was rapidly improving again. Perhaps it has fulfilled its original purpose and a new one is now developing.

We began to realise that the old energy within which many groups and individuals were doing good work was rapidly changing. Only those who were prepared to adjust to the new energy now developing would retain their importance and survive. Indeed I was beginning to feel that it was a question of not only moral but also physical survival; that we were entering a new era, that much that was happening was a preparation for a different mode of life we were about to enter.

We had promised ourselves a year of less work in order to gather our forces for whatever might be necessary, and to stop wasting our energy on small unimportant matters. We did not keep our promise.

Towards the end of the year we went to Brazil again.

CHAPTER 12

Problems with the Heart
The final lesson.

"Ah!"

"Why are you shouting?" my wife asked. She was driving her car near father-in-law's beach flat.

"Sorry, just a sudden pain."

It was the first of January 1994.

"Oh!"

I nearly dropped the cup of coffee I was holding in my left hand. Elizabeth got worried.

"Nothing much, just a pain going down my left arm."

I lay down. By now there was a pressure on my chest. I refused to accept that there was anything wrong. I had had such pains before. Elizabeth insisted on driving back to São Paulo. In the evening she cried.

"All right, tomorrow you can take me for an examination."

She drove me straight to the "Heart Hospital".

They could find nothing wrong with my heart, yet the pain did not stop in spite of injections which "always relieve the pain if coronary arteries are the cause", we were told. X-rays and ultrasound showed nothing. Before they did an angiogram, pushing a gadget into my heart and televising it whilst chemicals squirted into the coronaries, they felt a scintillographic examination (nuclear medicine) was advisable. But the machine had broken down.

"Let us forget all about it. I am always all right."

We went to another workshop which we thought might be useful, particularly for Elizabeth.

My pains though smaller continued. We went to the Albert Einstein hospital where the scintillographic equipment worked. Yes, there was a slight irregularity in my heart. So back to the "Heart Hospital" where a friend of Elizabeth was a cardiologist. An angiogram was performed. It was the first time that I was slightly afraid of the comparatively minor investigation. It was done using local anaesthetic. I did not watch the TV pictures showing the gadget being pushed through my arteries and finally the coronary arteries themselves. After I returned to the hospital room where I was going to spend the night together with Elizabeth, the cardiologist returned.

"I have looked at the film. Come along with me and I shall screen it for you and explain."

I think we both knew. He explained all we saw in detail. Elizabeth translated, until her voice suddenly choked. My Portuguese was just good enough.

"There is a constriction. The only way to remove it is by open heart surgery. A by-pass, at the back of the heart on a bend. No other way possible."

Elizabeth continued translating. "Brazil is a third world country. You may wish to be flown to England or the USA, but we have two good teams here. Think about it. Give me your answer tomorrow morning."

We thought about it. In an airplane anything can happen. One of the best heart surgeons happened to be a Brazilian. Elizabeth knew his daughter. She was more shocked by the diagnosis than I was. I believed absolutely that I had many more years of life. She needed the support of her family. We agreed that I should be operated on in São Paulo, provided that the top surgeon performed the operation.

I insisted he came personally and that I met him before he "cut out" my heart. There was a slight consternation in the eyes of my cardiologist. The surgeon was a busy man who operated in various hospitals and usually only looked at the angiogram, and arrived in the operating theatre after the patient's chest was opened. He had no time to see patients beforehand personally. But he came, explained to me the details in fluent English, was extremely polite and had his daughter telephone my wife.

Elizabeth had a change of clothes and a nightgown brought to her, and did not leave me for a minute, except to go to the toilet, from the moment the diagnosis was given. She even refused to go to the restaurant. Family and friends brought her food.

The next day I was given a premedical injection which was supposed to make me drowsy and relaxed for an hour or so before I was to be wheeled to the operating theatre.

Everything else also had been examined, liver, lungs, kidney, and even prostate, to make sure no unexpected emergency would occur during or after the operation. Even a psychiatrist who spoke fluent English came to examine me. Did they expect me to start beating up the nurses or surgeons during the operation? A third world country Brazil may be, but they were more thorough than in many an English hospital.

Four hours later the pre-med had completely worn off and they arrived to collect me. The surgeon had been held up by an operation which he had been performing in another hospital. Elizabeth walked at the side of the trolley on which I was being wheeled into the operating theatre. When we arrived, the anaesthetist and another nurse came to "welcome" us. They recognised Elizabeth from the time she used to work as an instrumental nurse. They suggested she scrubbed and watched the operation. She refused. To see her husband's heart being taken out was more than she felt she could take.

I was placed on the operating table. The lights were glaring. Several people in masks were doing something. I saw containers of what I thought must be blood, glistening knives, and other gadgets on a trolley. I was asked to sit up. Soon something pricked my back.

The next thing I noticed was a most unpleasant pain in my throat and a bright light. I remembered. I was warned that when I woke up a tube might still be in my throat pumping air into me so that I would breathe regularly. I was not to try and bite the tube! I waved my hands in the air to attract attention. There were several people lying close to me in the intensive care unit. A nurse arrived. I pointed at my throat, trying to imply that it hurt. They took the tube out gently. A female doctor arrived. In my usual way I turned my charm on and said, in what must have been a very peculiar voice, to say nothing of my Portuguese which was practically non-existent, that she was a very beautiful lady. I repeated similar compliments to several nurses. They wheeled me into a single room, surrounded by a glass wall, where I later realised they usually placed difficult or dying patients.

After a while I got bored and asked for a book to read and for my wife. This time they were really shocked. I was supposed to be only half-conscious or sleeping. They sent a clinical psychologist who spoke English and tried to make sure that my brain was not affected. At the same time they notified my wife who soon arrived carrying a book!

She told me that everything was all right. Somebody came out of the operating theatre every half hour or so to inform her of progress. Then one of the surgeons came just to tell me that the operation was a complete success. When Elizabeth left to get a little well-deserved sleep, I lifted my book so that I could see the pages between the various tubes pumping things into my body, and started reading. In spite of the clinical psychologist's diagnosis the nurses must have thought I was crazy.

My recovery was outstandingly fast for I was soon taken back to my room where Elizabeth was waiting for me. Ivani, a healing medium, came to see me with several other mediums in an endeavour to speed up my healing process. Somebody came and said that she saw several spirits in the operating theatre trying to help. A doctor friend of ours came and started channelling involuntarily. A nurse who came in during this time nearly dropped a tray with medications she was carrying and ran out of the room.

In "spiritual" matters Brazil is very different to Europe. I started walking a day after the operation and was taken to other patients to give them courage, and show them how quickly one can recover.

Seven days later I returned to my Brazilian home and rang my family in Europe to say that I was in perfect condition.

Towards the end of April '94 we met Daskalos, a Cypriot invited to Brazil by Zulma Reyo. Daskalos is probably the most important Christian esoteric philosopher of the twentieth century. Zulma is a friend of ours, who established "Alquimia" some eight years ago. After working in England, India, and the USA she felt that she had to establish in Brazil a group which would foster the "inner transformation" which many of us feel we are ready for. Amongst others she invites interesting, many of them prominent, people from abroad, who have special gifts. She has published several books.

Daskalos, whom Elizabeth and I were showing round São Paulo, had very poor eyesight, yet what he enjoyed most was looking at flowers in the botanical garden. They were too small for him to see with his "normal" eyes, but he said he saw them with his inner eye. He also said that he remembered well a previous incarnation when he was a child during the time of Jesus's life and crucifixion and had followed Jesus frequently. He explained to me several things in the New Testament which I did not understand. Most of them were either accidental or purposeful mistranslations according to him.

Soon after we met he said, "There is nothing wrong with your heart. Your operation was not really necessary." A few months later this was confirmed by Dr Nixon, a cardiologist in London. "But," he continued, "look after yourself." It was an enigmatic statement. I did not pursue it. Later Zulma told me that Daskalus had told her that if I did not change my style of life, if I did not look after myself and slow down, I should die soon, something confirmed later by Dr Nixon, though in less dramatic terms.

After we flew back to London in May my heart symptoms started again. Dr Nixon, the London cardiologist who had looked after my mother when she had a coronary, examined me and stated that my heart problems were due to tension and not cholesterol clogging up my coronary arteries. This tension caused wrong breathing resulting in a wrong carbon dioxide to oxygen mixture. All I had to do was get a lot of sleep, if necessary medicinally induced, for some time, relax completely and then learn to breathe correctly and try not to allow myself to become tense which resulted in hyperventilation.

This was not easy for me since though I could not work for anybody due to my various problems resulting from my accident, I knew I had to give advice and organise much which would be of benefit to some and hopefully to the world. I did what Dr Nixon advised, which included regular exercising, and have overcome my cardiac symptoms. I have given papers, published by Dr Nixon and others on whose work he based much of his theory and healing procedures, to other cardiologists. Though some had heard of his theories and techniques, and indeed a few agreed with them, very few were prepared to put them into practice. His methods require educating rather than medicating and operating on a patient. They are more time-consuming and certainly less profitable from a pharmaceutical point of view.

In a way I knew and had known for a long time much that mediums and now, on a different level, Dr. Nixon had told me. Both my mother and

I found that we sometimes knew things which logically we could not have known. On a physical level, I had had what Peter Nixon called a "coronary syndrome" before my accident and before he had reached his present conclusion as to the cause of these symptoms. I too knew the cause. I had been overworking myself. Somehow I had not been able or was not prepared to perceive it.

My whole heart affair taught me several things. The most superficial one was that I could overcome most physical difficulties because I was an optimist and believed, beyond any doubt, that I would survive. I was certain that most other people could do the same if they but chose to do so. I had been given a chance to remind myself of what I had learned after my accident. Then I wanted to walk, so I walked again.

But there was something deeper. The heart to me is associated with love. I believe that we have to learn something from every illness and difficulty.

My deep love for my surroundings was there, but respect and love for myself had to come later. I would try to attain it. To love those surrounding me was easy; to have more respect for my own limitations was more difficult. I loved life and myself, but in order to give to others I abused my body. I could but hope that I had learned my lesson and would not need another reminder.

It was also a lesson in humility. I had to learn that I had a human body which could only take a certain amount of abuse. I was not superman.

We also had to find more time for relaxation and not have our house full of guests all the time.

After my consultation with Dr Nixon, who advised complete rest, I had to be in the hospital for some ten days to get it, but when I left I could not go home since it was full of charming people. I had to go and stay with a friend, who lived alone, to get the peace I needed. Elizabeth, the ideal wife, was also completely exhausted, from visiting me every day whilst I was in hospital and later at my friend's house, and at the same time looking after our guests at home, showing them round and giving them the advice they needed. She might be nineteen years younger than I, but I had to think of her, only human, body as well.

CHAPTER 13

The All-Pervasive Knowledge
To know is good and the responsibility is an honour.

I want to become a medium. If I gain the ability I shall be able to help others to accept much that I feel should be accepted by most of humanity.

It was August 1994 and only a short time after my heart problem.

"Why do you think you can do more than other mediums can do?" Elizabeth asked.

"Because I am a scientist and most mediums are not trained in logical thought. I shall know better what questions to ask whatever energy it is that seems to speak through mediums. I am also a scientist with several degrees; people may take me more seriously than the usual mediums who have little or no higher education, in particular the scientific and perhaps the economic spheres." There was still much conceit left in me.

"If you feel you are ready then try it."

I went to the College of Psychic Studies which by now I knew well and asked to speak to Tony Neate, a medium more or less my age, and discussed my intention with him. Why I picked him I have no idea. He suggested some mediums who ran Development Courses as they were called. One attended for an evening once a week. He also said that in a centre which he and three other families ran, Runnings Park in Malvern, he with some of the others would run a Development or Channelling Course as he called it, lasting three long weekends. This appealed to me more. I was in a hurry.

Runnings Park is beautifully positioned in the country, near the border of Wales some three hours from London, and includes a hotel, restaurant and swimming pool. Many forms of natural treatment are also available, including massage, reflexology and a flotation tank, as well as counselling, hypnosis and spiritual healing. Anybody can go there and make use of the services offered, or just relax and enjoy the lovely countryside,

Chapter 13

clean air, small but comfortable rooms and good food.

Elizabeth agreed to join me. The other participants ranged from a Jumbo Jet pilot (a delicate woman who was also a painter!) through businessmen, an architect, a scientist to a spiritual healer and a housewife.

The first weekend was for us very relaxing. The participants, atmosphere, tutors and geographic surroundings were pleasant. We learned nothing new as regards the existence of chakras, auras, spirits, or energies as I prefer to call them. What I did find fascinating was the following demonstration.

Each of us put a personal object, a ring, watch, brooch and so on, into a sack. Nobody saw what anybody else put into it. Then each of us picked one of these objects out of the sack and said something about the person to whom it belonged. The idea was that we should not use any logical thought, just say the first things that came to our mind. We were not meant to look at the object. I picked what was obviously a belt. I said that it belonged to a fat person who threw out his/her legs and was perhaps a dancer, and some other things which I have forgotten. Then I realised that it was a short belt so could not belong to a fat person. It belonged in fact to an extremely slim lady who had intestinal problems, that is why I felt that it belonged to a fat or bloated person. She also loved dancing. I was not yet good enough to differentiate between real fatness and perceived fullness resulting from illness. Most other things also agreed. The person who picked my signet ring said that it belonged to a person who probably teaches and likes standing on a stage delivering speeches. All true of me. Most of us said things which were true of the person whose object they picked.

During the second weekend Elizabeth perceived during the night a shiver going through her, opened her mouth and tried to wake me up but no words came. It frightened her. When at last she could speak she woke me up. She was told that this is frequently the case when an outside energy tries to speak through a person who is not yet used to this phenomenon.

During the third weekend we were at one stage separated into groups of about four or five and asked to permit thoughts to come to us and voice them.

We had been warned before to protect ourselves by imagining a white light, or golden sphere or egg, surrounding us and if we felt any outside

165

energy approaching to challenge it, and permit only positive evolved energies to speak through us. When a person started speaking another member of the group was supposed to "cover" him, i.e. surround him with loving thoughts.

To my surprise it was I who spoke first. It was the 7th of December 1994. I saw earthquakes which occurred in January 1995 in Japan and Central America. I saw floods which occurred in February 1995 in Central Europe and in São Paulo.

Since then I have frequently known of things which would occur. Sometimes the timing was correct. Sometimes not. The two earthquakes in Greece I saw more or less correctly, but expected a third which did not happen. I forecasted the day on which the earthquake in West Turkey would occur. It occurred three weeks later.

This and many other things I seemed to know about future occurrences convinced me that we can only see the probable future, and never be absolutely certain. I used to record everything I saw or "just knew" onto a tape (I nearly always carry a recorder with me) and give a copy of the tape, if it concerned a person, to that person. Often I was right, but sometimes only nearly right.

I now believe that at best we can only know what the likelihood of future occurrences is in the energetic conditions as they are now. The energy may change due to other people's action and due to the use of our own Free Will. Should I ever be told that I will have a car accident tomorrow then I shall use my Free Will and not leave the house on that day. I could of course have a car accident on the following day and a general pattern may be predetermined, but I might also sidestep something completely by determined action of my Free Will.

The Free Will is what makes us different from machines. A pendulum will swing to and from, the hands of a clock will turn round and round. We can decide to do or not do something. Various possibilities are given to us. It is our choice that matters. I think that is what is meant when the Bible says, "Many are called but few are chosen."

One of the more interesting general things I saw initially was that 1995 would be a year in which the meteorological conditions on a world-wide scale would be unusual. Maxima and minima of temperature would be reached in many parts which had not been attained before.

There would be prolonged heatwaves and droughts, but also unusually heavy rainfalls and floods where in the past they rarely occurred. There would be more volcanic action and earthquakes than there are on average, nothing very dramatic but enough for people to realise, if they were prepared to, that something unusual was happening. If they did perceive this, and changed their mode of behaviour, more "drama" would happen in the future, but not as much as would occur if they did not choose to heed this warning.

In practice the USA had the driest season on record and the hottest for over a hundred years. The weather in England was exceptionally hot and dry. New Zealand recorded -22° C, a very rare if not unique experience. In São Paulo, Brazil, it was +32° C in July in the middle of winter, the normal temperature being 8-20° C, and so on. In England and elsewhere little has been written about this world-wide phenomenon. There were articles explaining that as a result of the greenhouse effect, and the hole in the ozone layer, a slight warming of the average global atmosphere will occur, perhaps one quarter of a degree per year. Nothing to worry about. The warning we experienced was not taken seriously.

Since I had these "feelings", most of which were not clear enough to call "visions", I had read several books channelled by other mediums, Ken Carey and Julie Soskin amongst them, who also see "dramatic" changes occurring on our globe, both in the physical and mental-spiritual field.

I "saw" a "comet"(?) coming close to our earth. Julie Soskin speaks of a second sun. Many including myself "see" floods and the sea level rising. I used to feel that the high point of these changes would come towards the end of this century (the usual end-of-century, this time millennium, scares?). Now I see it in the first years of the next century. One of the Jewish legends says that within the generation in which the Jewish state is recreated (this occurred in 1948) dramatic world-wide changes will occur. The Mayan calendar sees a new era starting in 2012.

I choose not to rely on my or other people's predictions or vision absolutely, also choose to take them as a serious probability which we can alter, at least to an extent, by our own Free Will.

Another of my early tapes which I felt compelled to dictate, speaks about the effect of electromagnetic energy on people and other living and some "non-living" substances. These energies which emanate not only from high-tension electric cables but also TV and radio transmission aerials, electrical and electronic machinery, and cellular telephones, as well as electric clock radios if standing near the bed where one sleeps, can, I said, cause illness and tiredness in people; they can change or reduce the effect of medicines that are produced in surroundings of high electromagnetic fields and can cause physiological changes in all living matter in general.

Later I read an article about experiments performed at a university in England showing that the sort of electromagnetic effects we are all exposed to, do cause changes in living cells.

In Poland after an enormous transmission tower collapsed, people said they felt "better". This is of course no proof, as it may be a purely subjective feeling, but after a short time school children began to achieve better examination results.

I have also since learned that our earth emits a certain frequency which is called the Schuman resonance. This is a frequency of 7.83 hertz. It was found that people in space capsules who were not exposed to this frequency suffered from various negative effects. Scientists at NASA traced these effects to the lack of exposure to this frequency. They now build into space capsules emitters producing this frequency.

Other proof, though not yet sufficiently documented, indicates that patients who recovered well after an operation or chemical treatment, rapidly became worse again after being transferred to high-tech modern hospital beds. These beds have several motors built into them so that the patient can move himself into various positions and thus, it is hoped, feel more comfortable.

Another of the thoughts that "came to me", which I taped, was that in the past many mediums channelled what they considered to be spirits of people who had once lived. They sometimes spoke with peculiar accents, and often were indeed very useful in the advice they gave. As I understood my "thoughts", this form of communication would rapidly diminish. The energy which would let some mediums know and therefore express ideas which they could not know from what they had learned by "ordinary" means, would be the "All-Pervasive Energy" rather than aspects of this energy as represented by what we call "spirits". Again I found that the energy which spoke through Julie Soskin in one of her published books said something similar. She called it a "joint consciousness". The words used are the product of our brain, so different mediums may well use different words meaning the same thing.

Another tape emphasised that if mediums worked jointly it would be easier to pass information through them.

What to me seemed the most important "vision" which I received was that we should form "centres of retreat and regrowth". I quote my tape.

"These centres can be developed only through the co-operation of several people who will use them themselves at times when they feel that they want to renew themselves. Others should also be involved who at this stage do not feel the necessity for renewal, but think that in the near future they may feel that necessity, and moreover feel that in the years to come such centres could be necessary because from them will start, in a way, a new life, in the start of which they will cooperate. They know that this start is necessary because we have to continue with much that has been achieved to the present time, and that this should not be lost.

"Such centres should consist of people who have a spiritual background or know that they will have such a background even though they do not have it now. And also of people who have abilities which are useful on the earth plane, and have knowledge of developments that have taken place to date whether it is in the business or technological field. They must be prepared to give of themselves the knowledge which they possess to others, particularly when there will not be so many who have this knowledge, particularly during times of confusion.

"These centres may be primitive or not, it does not matter. They must be comfortable enough for the people building them now to wish to spend frequently some time there. A time during which they can enjoy themselves, relax and also absorb deeper energies which for the time being will help them in the world as it is now; and later will help them to act in the world as it will be, very different to the present world.

"Some of them should have not only knowledge of higher technology but simple down-to-earth technical knowledge, so that when things break down they can repair them and thus continue a life somewhat similar to the present one.

"People should not shy away from such centres because they bring no financial profit now, or be afraid that other people will not come to them now because they are too primitive or not comfortable enough. Those who are prepared to help in the development of the future will accept those centres even if they do not have the comfort to which we are used.

"The functioning of these centres should be independent of external power such as electricity. They should produce or be prepared to produce their own. They should have their own supplies of all that is necessary to sustain life, in particular their own water. It will be a pleasure, even now, to be in a place which one knows to be independent of the highly polluted energy.

"Business people as well as simple people will cooperate with pleasure in building such centres; once just a few, perhaps only three or four, start such work, within a few years and with just a little bit of sacrifice, more finance will come, to each centre differently. All of those who start these things know that the finances for the necessary day-to-day expenses will come when really necessary, provided that the people are convinced that they will come.

"These centres should be in a peaceful area, not polluted by excessive sound, near forests, hills, mountains, not too close to the sea, preferably away from large conglomerations of people. Small towns, villages are all right, but away from conglomerations of hundreds of thousands of people, because these large conglomerations cause much pollution. Few such places can be found, but they exist. They must not be so far away that people cannot come to them regularly, whenever they need a few days at a time or perhaps a month or two of respite.

"Sometimes I see barracks, mainly wooden structures. Sometimes, I see white stone structures. They must be easily repairable, not so light that they will be moved by strong gusts of wind. They must be easily protected from aggressive people, and animals. Certainly they must be able to withstand natural disasters, rains. They should be capable of expansion even in the last moments. In the last moment more people will want to be there, but only people of sufficiently high elevation will really want to come. Others will probably not want to come because they will not think them comfortable enough.

"Multinational groupings are to be aimed for but it is not vital. Certainly the right people should be there. Not all of the same background, not all thinking that only one path is the right path, but the overall path must be accepted. The details as to how to go along this path may vary. We are all different genetically and that is good, that is the way it ought to be, and therefore there will be differences in the way we want to develop.

"Even different languages will not slow down development, because the language which we speak, with our voices, will become less important. We will reach a level where we can communicate with each other in different ways in the near future.

"There should be no leaders, no one dictates how to develop, it has to be a joint development. The time of gurus has passed, now many of us can feel what should be done. We should decide jointly.

"Only those groups which can decide jointly will flourish and prosper. Only from those groups can development come again. There will be no poverty because those groups are rich in thought. Therefore richness in physical aspects will also come. This is necessary for us, but must not be of primary importance. Spiritual and physical richness jointly is the right way. Each of us who wants to join in creating such a centre will be able to suggest one or two others who will be prepared to help in the co-creation.

"What is the good of great wealth which many of us have, if that wealth is going to bring us nothing or little in the future. It is clear that it is good to use some of this wealth now, even if we do not believe in the different times that will come (we have an idea that they might come). Being as we are, we are only prepared to use some of our wealth to create something which is going to be an investment in the future, a sort of box for safety, a box for emergencies. Many of us will accept this necessity, because they know that even if they do not have to dip into this emergency box, it is there and gives one a comfortable feeling.

"And perhaps because of that peaceful feeling, things will not be as difficult as they would be if we did not have that feeling of confidence.

"Nothing is certain, nothing can be forecast with detailed certainty. The more of us are prepared for difficult times, the less difficult they might be for the majority, not only for those who are prepared for them.

"The important thing is to believe in the future and that we all have a duty to the future. To know that the future is us. Without us there is no future. So let us make ourselves places where we can refuel, recharge, and at the same time know that in emergencies we can survive there for long periods of time, until we can expand from there again into the beauties around us.

"Never be afraid of what the future might bring. Whatever it brings is right. The only thing to fear is whether we are prepared right now, to do what is right.

"The future is variable, the past was, there is nothing we can do about it. All we can change and do, is to work with the present. So let us concentrate on it and do what we know is the right thing to do at the present time.

"Some of us will think that the right thing to do is make more money. If this is what they think, let them do it. They cannot do anything else. But many will know that if they are sufficiently well off, then just as it is good to spend some money on a holiday, on enjoying oneself on drinking a bottle of wine, so it is good to spend some on a place which is not just a retreat, but which is a place for the future. There is no need to persuade others of the truth of this, but there is a need to mention it to others. If deep down they are ready and know that it is correct, it will trigger a reaction in them and they will join. If they are not yet ready, maybe they will be ready next year.

"Those of us who know this should not be ashamed to talk about it. Not insist, but talk; it will have an effect. They should not be ashamed or afraid. If it is accepted that is good enough.

"Nearly all those Elizabeth and Tadeusz know are interested in this because that is the way it is meant to be. Those who waver can be influenced by these two, because they have a great power of influencing without insisting, because they are catalysts. People will follow them. It is not a question of following a leader, just of accepting some ideas. People who are deeply happy have ideas; these ideas are usually correct.

"Sometimes mistakes can be made even by people who are happy; that is where others come in and correct them.

"Greenery, high places, water, simple windmills, watermills, peaceful surroundings, grazing and agricultural land, above all good will, will be achieved and that soon. It has to be started now. The proof that it has to be started now will come very soon.

"There will be destruction in some places; it would be better if it did not come, but some has to come to show the necessity of what has to be done. There will be howling winds, big waves. How much destruction will occur depends on us. We can avoid much of it but not all.

"There is an All-Pervasive Energy. Many of us can perceive it. There is no need for it now to come via 'spirits'; this only causes distortion. It is better if it comes directly to a person. A simple story repeated by other people becomes distorted. If we accept it directly it is much better. All can do it!

"Tadeusz, work with others and you will understand better. You are working alone and that is difficult. Work with others who work in groups and can therefore do it better."

Early in 1995 I shared this "vision" with Dr Raul Correa, a Brazilian scientist, and several of my wife's family, particularly Alvaro, my wife's brother, his wife Lilian and their daughters. Raul and I drew up an outline proposal for the formation of an Institute which would foster the co-operation between the orthodox and unorthodox, between ancient wisdom and modern technology and the possible establishment of a teaching centre or university. The requirement that this centre and a community be established outside a main town on high ground with its own water supply, the possibility of growing our own unpolluted food, producing our own power from wind, water and sun was a prerequisite.

In April 1995 some twenty of us met to discuss these proposals.

I explained that the basic idea was not only to form a self-sufficient community to which any of us and others could go for relaxation, and where those of us who wished to could have their own houses, but to establish a centre of learning, research, and production of medicines and other chemicals from locally available materials, where others could come, learn and spread our knowledge. I also felt strongly that the centre which we would establish should be in contact with other centres in the world which I was certain would be established.

My Portuguese was still weak; my wife, the best wife in the world, at least for me, had to translate.

The enthusiasm was incredible. There and then "Instituto Atalanta" was born.

The name Atalanta came to Raul. When I looked it up in encyclopaedias I found that Atalanta was in ancient mythological history a goddess who ran very fast. Any god who could catch her could have a child with her. These children became the gods of the Greeks. In alchemy Atalanta was the chrysalis from which the butterfly emerges. We adopted the symbol, the Greek L as its logo. Months later a friend told me that all Greek and Hebrew letters had a meaning. The meaning of this one was "learning".

Our dream had become a reality.

All we have to do is suspend our doubts and distractions, and believe and be prepared to sacrifice for this belief what has to be sacrificed, and it will happen.

Love is the basic building block towards a path to light.

APPENDIX 1

ATALANTA INSTITUTE
For the Integration of Humanity

The Institute became a reality in April 1995, but bureaucracy took until 6th December 1995 before it was officially born. This was the day on which I gave my first lecture to members and friends of the Institute after returning from Europe. Whilst there we not only purchased some 50 kg of books, dealing with technical details of how to build wind and water mills, solar panels, utilise waste products, etc., all necessary when establishing a healthy self-sufficient community, but also talked to many people who felt that similar centres ought to be established in other countries.

Since May 1995 the Institute has given many lectures and workshops at its present residence in São Paulo. It has now purchased 250 acres of land with beautiful views, its own springs and waterfall some 100 km north of São Paulo and has started building a self-sufficient centre with all the amenities it intended. Many donations are still required to complete the work.

Since the book was first written, Atalanta has started building and planting on its grounds. Anybody interested in further details should contact:

Atalanta, Rua Francisco Dias Velho 95/51, São Paulo-SP, 04581-000, Brazil;

Fax: +55 (0)11 5097 9559;

e-mail: degromoboy@aol.com

Or: Atalanta, Caixa Postal 41, Extrema-MG, 37640-000, Brazil.

Fax: (+55) (0)35 3435 2033

Atalanta has also been registered in England with Dr Jeremy Birnstingl, an environmental scientist, as its secretary.

Below is a statement of the reasons for the existence of the Institute as given initially to its existing and prospective members, followed by a copy of a statement of intent produced by Dr Birnstingl of Atalanta UK in 1998. It will be adopted by all Atalanta centres.

ATALANTA INSTITUTE
For the Integration of Humanity

The reasons for its existence examined under the following headings:
1. The present world situation
2. Its objectives
3. First actions
4. General development

The basis of its existence is trust and respect amongst all those participating in its activities. Atalanta is a charitable institute which has no leaders, masters or gurus. Dr Tadeusz and Mrs Elizabeth de Gromoboy Dabrowicki, Dr Raul Correa Filho, Mr Alvaro and Mrs Lilian Restaino are the founders of the Institute.

THE PRESENT WORLD SITUATION

RESTLESSNESS
An increasing number of people are becoming aware of their own power and knowledge, that gurus are a symptom of the past, that governments have become excessively bureaucratic, and that they can no longer wait in some cases for governments to take action.

A restlessness is developing in most known communities, demanding a new approach to life. The findings of physics, chemistry, psychology, mysticism and religion are coming together into a new synthesis.

DEMAND FOR RELAXATION AND UNDERSTANDING
An increasing number of people in medium and high-level positions in business, society, industry and even politics, feel the need for a rest from the current work in surroundings which offer something different from

their usual hotels or beach houses. An increasing number also feel that they would like to know a little more about "spiritual" matters, not necessarily from conventional sources. They feel there is something more than what the various formalised religions offer. This was the case in the 15th century when the Reformation developed and a large number of different religious approaches were then created. This time they are searching for a unified new approach. The question "Why do we live?" is becoming increasingly important, and not "How can I live more comfortably?"

CHAOS AND DRAMATIC CHANGES

The possibility of a period of chaos is not only arising in people's minds, but is also discussed as a distinct possibility in scientific, economic, popular and esoteric literature.

The current main source of power is fossil fuel, which is being exhausted. Atomic power is as yet potentially dangerous. The by-products of both are polluting the world to unacceptable levels. Their effects on meteorological conditions are becoming noticeable. Weather patterns are changing.

During 1995 there were on average throughout the world greater extremes in temperature, rain and drought than in recorded history. It is obvious to those who are prepared to face the fact, whether validated or not, that the destruction of the ozone layer as well as ground pollution will cause in the next few years even greater changes, including the melting of some of the ice cap, thus raising the sea level, and that some disruption of our present mode of life is inevitable.

SCIENTIFIC SCEPTICISM VERSUS INTUITIVE KNOWLEDGE

Scientific scepticism which demands solid evidence about any new assertion, and how it works, and which rejects intuitive knowledge even if statistically proven, is no longer accepted by an increasing proportion of humanity as the best way to progress.

HEALING, ORTHODOX AND ALTERNATIVE MEDICATION

The side effects and by-products of many chemicals and medicines are becoming so noticeable that an increasingly large section of the population is turning to alternative medication and healing, as well as to ecologically acceptable products.

ELECTROMAGNETIC POLLUTION

Many scientists and others are realising that electromagnetic pollution caused by high-tension cables, many machines, radio and TV transmission waves, cellular telephones, etc., is reaching unacceptable levels.

It has recently been shown by university research in several countries that exposure to the sort of EM waves many of us are constantly exposed to causes changes in biological cells and major health problems.

ECONOMIC STRUCTURE

The large differences in wages between the upper, middle and lower classes of society in the third world are no longer acceptable. They lead to distrust and low, inefficient production, as well as to corruption, burglary and low levels of education.

The present economic structure based purely on profit and multinational companies appears to many no longer to be viable.

The world-wide economic depression is showing no sign of ending. This in itself is causing and will continue to cause more chaos.

INTUITIVE REALISATION

The intuitive realisation many have come to is that we have reached the end of an epoch and that the way ahead lies in a dramatic change of attitude if the world, as we know it, is not to be destroyed. Fears are expressed that meteorological, geological or cosmically caused cataclysms can occur, or that such cataclysms may be caused by over-population, pollution or lack of consideration for our neighbours.

OBJECTIVES

Establishment of centres where the above ideas are discussed and acted upon in the manner outlined below.

One or more centres in the country which will be self-sufficient, capable of supplying their own healthy, non-polluted food and water supply, as well as producing their own electrical power and heating by utilising the wind, water, sun and where possible thermal gradients and other natural forms of energy.

One or more centres in towns where lectures and workshops can be given.

The centres in the country to be used for:

1. Relaxation, meditation and healing by non-invasive techniques. People may wish to stay there for brief, medium or long periods. Some may wish to establish their second or main home there.

2. The holding of conferences, teaching and spreading of knowledge acquired in the centre. In particular the use of natural energy and medication, and most importantly the synergetic form of life practised there whilst researching and propagating synergetic and ecological ideas in political and economic fields.

3. Production of medicines and other chemicals from currently growing plants.

4. Construction of machines and tools for the production of power from natural resources, their storage and information on where they are available.

5. Re-establishment of various ancient and traditional forms of knowledge and wisdom in the light of recently acquired knowledge, particularly in the field of healing of body and soul. Use of meditative and body-manipulative as well as medicinal techniques.

6. Establishment of a library and reference centre for the above.

7. Helping communities near the seat of the Institute Centre and encouraging the human community of the world to work in greater collaboration.

8. Furthering the learning of a single world language.

9. Encouragement of intuitive work, not in following any particular religion but in a general perception of energies not yet explicable by orthodox science.

All the above points to be established on three levels:

I. Research: including national and international meetings, and conferences of those possessing a high knowledge in relevant fields.

II. The teaching of this knowledge to those who feel they wish to acquire it.

III. The spreading of this knowledge to the surrounding area, and Brazil in particular, but the world in general in a compassionate manner.

PRACTICAL PROCEDURE:

1. Obtaining land, preferably in a mountainous area with a waterfall, running water and land usable for agricultural purposes of at least 800,000 sq. m. More land should be available for acquisition nearby, well away from large population centres and flight paths.

2. Erection of prefabricated (or not, depending on finance available, cost and speed of erection) buildings to house:

1st Stage:
a)   50 guests in individual or attached chalets.
b)   Conference centre for 100 participants.
c)   Library with video and sound facilities with individual earphones.
d)   Workshops for tool, etc., production and repair.
e)   Meditation centre (multi-purpose).
f)   Body treatment rooms.
g)   Medical surgery.
h)   Small laboratory for medical tests, orthodox and complementary.

i)   Laboratory for preparation of medicines, herbal, homeopathic, etc.
j)   Four or more family chalets for permanent staff and those intimately involved.
k)   Kitchen and restaurant for guests and residents.
l)   Two lounges for discussion.
m)   A classroom.

3 Establishment of:
• Windmill and watermill for production of electricity.
• Solar panels for production of hot water.
• Solar panels for production of electricity.
• Fresh water well and pump or clean water from mountain brook.
• On site or nearby: chemical laboratories, production units and mechanical laboratories.

Expansion of the centre must be easy.
   Some ground to be used for the planting of medicinal plants, and some for the planting of vegetables and fruit for local use. No artificial fertilisers to be used. No pollution by chemicals or noise and only minimally by electromagnetic waves must be the aim.

FIRST ACTIONS

Workshops and lectures by people who have a deep knowledge of a given field, e.g.:

1. The probable near future changes which may occur in both the physical and economic states of the world. Such knowledge may have been acquired by scientific or intuitive means.

2. Body and soul healings.

3. Use of alternative forms of energy, such as wind, water and sun.

4. Reasons why herbal, homeopathic, acupressure, etc., types of healing are often preferable to drug and invasive healing.

5. Stress relief.

The lectures should initially be of a type that easily attract large audiences.

Conferences:

1. Production of medication from plants.

2. Production of electrical and heat energy from natural sources.

3. Healing by non-orthodox methods.

4. Production of fuel from plants.

5. Alternative compassionate and intuitive management to achieve higher efficiency.

6. "Doctor-healer" or "Orthodox-unorthodox healing".

7. English Courses - residential complete immersion.

GENERAL DEVELOPMENT
The workshops and lectures, as well as the conferences, should be events lasting three days or more and be advertised as being so arranged as to give the participants relaxation and inspiration, with massage, etc., being available in their spare time. Participants should be encouraged to come a day earlier or stay a day longer to relax and look through the library if they wish.

At the same time the centre should be advertised as a self-contained unit for relaxation with alternative healing available if required, away from all noise and stress, in healing surroundings where visitors can have a glimpse of an alternative future. A library containing books not only on scientific, and alternative developments, but also of ancient and traditional approaches, and their synthesis with modern work, in medical, scientific, economic, social and political fields, should also contain the various predictions for the future offered by scientists, economists and those based on ancient documents and recent mediumistic statements

There should be tapes, sound and video of lectures and conferences given.

In the near future, the teaching and the research aspects should be developed into a form of alternative university. Therefore, some founder members of the institute should have an interest in and experience of academic work. They should have suitable academic qualifications.

My Beautiful World

STATEMENT OF INTENT
by Dr Jeremy Birnstingl

ATALANTA...

Aims to realise the vision of Sustainable Fulfilled Living through demonstrating, facilitating and encouraging the application of three simple principles:

- Sustainability
- Practicability
- Spirituality

to any sphere of action

WHY?

We don't have to look far to realise that some changes are needed in our personal lives, in society, and in our treatment of our environment, if the future is going to be an improvement on the present, or even be there at all for us.

But we have a great deal of vested interests in the systems we presently live in, and our human world marches on with seemingly unstoppable inertia.

So if we can't stop the train, we need to change the points, and divert it to the destination we all would like: a long and happy future, sustainable, Fulfilled Living.

The change must come willingly, enthusiastically, from within each individual and organisation. For this to happen, it must be simple, attractive and congruent with our needs.

The Atalanta Principles can be used by anyone, and provide a simple checklist for achieving the vision. Each requires specific thought and creative application in each situation in question.

Developing anything in accordance with the Atalanta Principles, be it a lifestyle, relationship, business or building, will help ensure its long and happy future, Sustainable and Fulfilled Living.

SPIRITUAL...

In harmony with nature (both inner and outer), integrating, ethical, appealing, refreshing, imparts a deep feeling of purpose and value, delights the spirit, supportive of evolution and betterment, caring, all-inclusive/non-exclusive, wholesome, good, loving respectful, enjoyable.

PRACTICAL...

Fulfils a purpose, need or requirement, does a job, convenient, simple, clear, easy to use, grounded, it works!

SUSTAINABLE...

Meets present needs without compromising future needs, balanced, no net depletion of resources, no net accumulation of wastes, enjoyable, common sense, economically viable, adaptable, flexible.

ALL THREE MUST BE PRESENT!

APPENDIX 2

Addresses

Atalanta (Brazil)

Rua Francisco Dias Velho 95/51,
São Paulo-SP
04581-000
Brazil
      Fax: +55 (0) 11 5097 9559
      e-mail: degromoboy@aol.com
      Atalanta, Caixa Postal 41, Extrema-MG, 37640-000, Brazil.
      www.geocities.com/RainForest/Vines 2628

Atalanta (UK)

Dr Jeremy Birnstingl
11 Greenwood House,
31 Princes Way,
London SW19 6QH
United Kingdom
      Tel/Fax: +44 (0) 20 8789 8418
e-mail: jbirnstingl@aol.com

Denny Dakin
Squirrel Cottage
Springfield Lane
Broadway
Worcestershire WR12 7BT
United Kingdom
      Tel/Fax: +44 (0) 1386 853043

David Lindsay
Flat 1,
96 Ifield Road,
London SW10 9AD
United Kingdom
     Tel: +44 (0) 20 7351 3547

General

Alquimia (Brazil)
R: Antonio De Macedo Soares, 1562
04607-003
São Paulo-SP
Brazil
     Tel: +55 (0) 11 241 3013
     Fax: +55 (0) 11 240 5149
e-mail: alquimiainterior@alquimiainterior.com.br
www.alquimiainterior.com

College of Psychic Studies
16 Queensbury Place
London SW7 2EB
United Kingdom
     Tel: +44 (0) 20 7589 3292
     Fax: +44 (0) 20 7589 2824
e-mail: cpstudies@aol.com
www.psychic-studies.org.uk

Friedborn Sanatorium (Germany)
Brigitte Greim
Lehnhof 4
79736 Rickenbach
Germany
     Tel: +49 (0) 7765 240
     Fax: +49 (0) 7765 8330

e-mail: Klinik.Friedborn@t-online.de
www.friedborn.de

Elizabeth de Gromoboy
50 Abinger Road
London W4 1EX
        Tel: +44 (0) 20 8994 1195
        Fax: +44 (0) 20 8995 5164

and

Rua Francisco Dias Velho 95/51
Brooklin - São Paulo - SP
04581 000
Brazil
Tel: +55 (0) 11 5543 1707
     +55 (0) 11 5542 5112
Fax: +55 (0) 11 5097 9559

Runnings Park
(Hotel and Tony Neate)
Croft Bank
West Malvern
Worcestershire WR14 4BP
United Kingdom
        Tel: +44 (0) 1684 573 868
        Fax: +44 (0) 1624 892 047
e-mail: info@runningspark.co.uk

Baroness Edmée di Pauli
31 Grove End Road
London NW8 9LY
        Tel: +44 (0) 20 7286 4287
e-mail: edmee.dipauli@talk21.com

Scientific and Medical Network
Gibliston Mill
Colinburgh
Leven
Fife KY9 1JS
Scotland
United Kingdom
> Tel: +44 (0) 1333 340 492
> Fax: +44 (0) 1333 340 491
e-mail: dl@scimednet.org
www.scimednet.org

Society for Psychical Research
49 Marloes Road
London W8 6LA
United Kingdom
> Tel: +44 (0) 20 7937 8984

Julie Soskin
The School of Insight and Intuition
Midford, Uxbridge Rd,
Hampton
Middlesex TW12 1BD
> Tel: +44 (0) 20 8979 0940
> Fax: +44 (0) 20 8255 8303
e-mail: insight@axiom.co.uk
www.insightandintuition.com

Rosemary Steel
51 Rushton Road
Desborough
Kettering NN14 2RP
United Kingdom
> Tel: +44 (0) 1536 762 706

INDEX OF KEY PHENOMENA